SIMPLY SOPHISTICATED

SIMPLY
Sophisticated

What
Every
Worldly
Person
Needs to
Know

by
Suzanne Munshower

THE SUMMIT GROUP • FORT WORTH, TEXAS

THE SUMMIT GROUP

1227 West Magnolia, Suite 500, Fort Worth, Texas 76104

Printed in the United States of America

10 9 8 7 6 5 4 3 2

ISBN: 1-56530-148-X $12.95

Book design by David Sims
Illustrations by Gorland Mor

Contents

Acknowledgments..vii

Introduction...ix

1 The Sophisticated Shopper 1

2 The Sophisticated Sipper 21

3 The Sophisticated Gourmet...............................45

4 The Sophisticated Investor................................71

5 The Sophisticated Aesthete 81

6 The Sophisticated Listener 95

7 The Sophisticated Viewer.................................109

8 The Sophisticated Sport 125

9 The Sophisticated Driver.................................135

10 The Sophisticated Reader.................................141

11 The Sophisticated Linguist..............................151

12 The Sophisticated Traveler 163

Acknowledgments

With appreciation to Mike Towle, Susan Besze Wallace, and, especially, the ultra-sophisticated Julie Logan.

Sophistication
and You

We all might wish to be thought of as sophisticated, but ask us to define this quality called "sophistication" and we're more likely than not to let out a very *unsophisticated* "Huh?"

What *is* sophistication?

We all pretty much recognize it when we see it, but—like the color *puce**—it's not so easy to describe. (In case you *don't* know the color puce when you see it, it's a brownish purple. *Puce* being French for "flea," you can imagine the glorious hue.) In fact, many dictionaries tend to define sophistication in terms of what it emphatically *isn't.*

Sophistication means being *not* artless, *not* simple, *not* naïve. Sophisticates aren't born, they're made. Which means that you, too, can become one.

The truth is, most of us *want* to be considered sophisticated. We don't want to be perceived as raw, unfinished material. We long for recognition for our worldliness, dreading the idea of people looking at us as if we just fell off the back of the proverbial turnip truck.

And why shouldn't we crave sophistication? We know much of life's success depends on something as quixotic as the ability to discern between a *crème brûlée** and cream of wheat. We realize that sophistication is the key not only to appreciation of the finer things in life but also to the inlaid mahogany desk and windowed corner suite.

We are constantly being judged by our sophistication or lack of it. If you're sitting on a big enough pile of money or wielding the sort of power usually associated only with Third World dictators or Hollywood studio heads, few will be brave enough to snicker as you order a bottle of "From Our Feet To Your Lips" wine or roll their eyes when you declare your favorite classical composer to be Andrew Lloyd Webber. On the other hand, if you're just plain folk, you'd better start getting fancy.

The aim of *Simply Sophisticated* is to increase your level of sophistication. The great thing about sophistication is: As you acquire the knowledge that allows you to *pass* as a sophisticate, you actually *become* one.

Sophistication is not about flaunting obscure knowledge. The cultured and sophisticated despise a showoff as much as their country cousins. This is not *The Parvenu's Handbook* or *The A To Z of Social Climbing*, though there's undoubtedly a market for both.

Sophistication is not about manners. It's certainly possible to be sophisticated yet rude, just as it is to be both vulgar and boring. Some people actually manage to be all four. Consider Madonna.

Sophistication also is not about trendiness. Sophistication does have its trends, but trendiness in itself is not sophistication. For example, tattoos and Harley Davidsons are not, and never will be, sophisticated, no matter who wears or rides them. On the other hand, cigarette smoking, which was considered the height of sophistication fifty and sixty years ago, and even inspired its own sleek satin and velvet jackets, is now taboo.

By now you might be asking, "So what do I get for my thirteen bucks?" What you get is that all-important component of sophistication called *savoir-faire**, which literally means "to know how." *Savoir-faire* is that quality of emanating worldliness.

As much an attitude as an ability, sophistication is acquired only through picking up a little baggage along the way. Luckily, the baggage of sophistication is useful and life enhancing. This also is what sets sophistication apart

Publisher's Note:
Pronunciation keys for some of the more difficult words, names, and phrases will be provided at the end of each chapter in a section called "The Articulate Sophisticate." Terms included in these pronunciation guides will be marked in the text with an asterisk. These pronuciations were researched by the author and her research staff to the best of their abilities, although some of these terms are pronounced differently in different parts of the world. Every effort has been made to provide the pronunciations most widely used.

from simple social climbing. Knowing the names of the *Blue Book* society families and whether they summer on the Cape, Shelter Island, or Newport won't do a thing to improve your life unless you're selling one of those bargains the rich just can't resist—like those light bulbs

SOPHISTICATED	NOT
The South of France	South Dakota
Picasso	Peter Max
Champagne and caviar	Corned beef and cabbage
Wolfgang Amadeus Mozart	Barry Manilow
Gianni Versace*	Sergio Valente
Tiffany	Monet
Filofax	Address book
Manolo Blahnik* mules	Dr. Scholl's sandals
Risotto*	Rice-a-Roni
Polo	Ping Pong
Muscadet*	Muscatel
Personal shoppers	Home shopping networks
Microfiber	Polyester
Big German cars	Big American cars
Orlando, the film	Orlando, the town
Gelato*	Dairy Queen
Meat loaf and mashed potatoes	Meat loaf and mashed potatoes

guaranteed not to burn out during anyone's natural lifetime. Unless you've got a quarter for the ferry, such knowledge won't even get you to Staten Island. On the other hand, learning a bit about art, knowing how to handle a wine list, gaining appreciation of *haute cuisine**, mastering the lingo of finance, or being able to distinguish between Louis Vuitton* and Leonardo da Vinci can add richness to your life and safeguard you from lifelong embarrassment.

So, to get back to the question of what sophistication *is*, it's that blend of grace and knowledge and that certain *je ne sais quoi* * that once separated the rubes from the royals and that now divides those who *are* cosmopolitan from those who read *Cosmopolitan*.

Simply Sophisticated will give you everything you need to pass yourself off as acceptably sophisticated in any group. It is to be hoped that,

SOPHISTICATED SYNONYMS

Fifteen Adjectives for the New You

Artful
Citified
Complex
Cosmopolitan
Cultivated
Elaborate
Experienced
Knowing
Lacking natural simplicity
Not naïve
Pertaining to fashionable life
Refined
Seasoned
Urbane
Worldly

after reading this gentle primer, you'll go on your way fired with the desire to know more about some of the subjects herein. That, too, is quite simple. The world is filled with fine museums, concert halls, and libraries just as it abounds with snooty designer boutiques, haughty French restaurants, and snobbish purveyors of fine wines.

With *Simply Sophisticated*, not even the most condescending waiter will intimidate you. You'll be confident yet modest, polished yet never patronizing, refined yet reticent. You will be, in a word, a *sophisticate*.

THE ARTICULATE SOPHISTICATE

crème brûlée (krem broo-LAY)
gelato (zheh-LAH-toe)
Gianni Versace (JHAH-nee vehr-SAH-chee)
haute cuisine (oat kwee-ZEEN)
je ne sais quoi (jhuh neh say QWAH)
Louis Vuitton (LOO-ee vwee-TOHN)
Manolo Blahnik (mah-NO-loe BLAH-nik)
Muscadet (moose-kah-DAY)
puce (pyooce)
risotto (ree-SEW-toe)
savoir-faire (sav-waar FAIR)

Chapter One

Shopper

Though most sophisticates love to shop, there exist many variations on the theme. There is, of course, the Jet Set Shopper, who travels to Europe for the *couture** shows, thinks nothing of dropping forty or fifty grand for a seasonal wardrobe, and will casually dismantle an ancient Continental château for reassembly in Grosse Pointe or Palm Beach. But, though these are the shoppers whose adventures fill the pages of *Town & Country* and *W*, they comprise a small group. Most sophisticated shoppers rely on their taste and ingenuity more than their bankrolls.

The Mall Sophisticate knows malls hold some great buys even the wealthy find chic and acceptable. The Mall Sophisticate loves popping into the Gap, Benetton (and its sister store, Sisley), Guess, Victoria's Secret, Compagnie Express, and other mall-based chain stores.

And why not buy your shoes at Leeds if they look like they came from Florence?

~

The Outlet Lover is a dedicated American outlet shopper who always seems to know where you can get something wholesale. On your way to Palm Springs? Don't forget to stop at the Joan and David shoe outlet. Touring Pennsylvania's Amish country? Don't pass up the Mark Cross and Calvin Klein outlets in Reading. Weekending in New York? New Jersey and the Donna Karan* outlet aren't far away, and there's every woman's favorite bargain box, the S & W store on Seventh Avenue—not to mention the designer bargains downtown on Orchard Street. Skiing in Colorado? Durango's Polo outlet is a must. The Outlet Lover has not one love but two: labels and low prices.

~

The Resale Shopper hangs out at designer resale boutiques hoping to pick up recognizably expensive designer clothing from Chanel*, Isaac Mizrahi*, Carolina Herrera, Moschino*, Gianni Versace, and other society favorites. Because he or she doesn't have the money to buy things new, compromises often are made. Result? The Resale Shopper is often a fashion victim, dressed in high-priced castoffs that convey a sense of status more than a flair for fashion.

~

The Design Maven cares about quality fabrics and the structural design of fashions, and wants style that's not only high, but also lasting. This shopper leans toward the new American classic designers—Calvin Klein, Donna Karan, Richard Tyler, Linda Allard for Ellen Tracy, Dana Buchman—and purchases "bridge" fashions in the under-$500-per-item range. Design Mavens also like the fashionable yet conservative lines of Emanuel by Ungaro and KL by Karl Lagerfeld, and the private label lines purveyed by Saks Fifth Avenue, Nordstrom, and I. Magnin. Striving Design Mavens dream of one day being able to plunk down $3,000 or $4,000 for a top-of-the-line suit by Richard Tyler or Jil Sander.

∾

The Trendsetter, who is really just a faster trend *follower*, hungers for the new and different and is a big fan of avant-garde designers. If money's an object, this shopper can be found haunting the sales at Neiman-Marcus, Saks Fifth Avenue, Bergdorf Goodman, Barney's, Bloomingdales, Maxfield in L.A., and Charivari in New York in search of marked-down fashions from Comme des Garçons, Issey Miyake*, Yohji Yamamoto*, Romeo Gigli, Isaac Mizrahi, Rifat Ozbek*, or Azzedine Alaïa*. If money's *not* an object, he or she can be found paying full price for the same clothes a month earlier.

∾

The Classic Shopper knows what he or she wants and will usually define the goal as "well-made things that never go out of style." This sophisticate rarely strays from the tried and true preppy look on his or her infrequent shopping trips to Brooks Brothers, J. Press, Ralph Lauren's flagship store on Madison Avenue, St. John knitwear departments, and Coach leather shops. The Classic Shopper likes antique furnishings and plain white cotton linens—and never ever gets rid of a sweater or a sofa until it's truly threadbare.

~

The Euro-Bargain Shopper will go to great lengths to have the right labels at the best prices and usually can be found on annual shopping jaunts to the countries that manufacture the products he or she holds dear.

If you can afford to drop several thousand dollars in one lump sum and refrain from shopping the rest of the year, this is a great way to get a European vacation *and* the best for less, as buying merchandise where it's manufactured can easily cut prices by 50 percent. Thus, a shopper's overseas agenda might include purchasing Yves St. Laurent ready-to-wear and Céline shoes in France, Bottega Veneta* and Gucci* leather goods in Italy, then going on to London to pick up a new Burberry raincoat and some bespoke Hilditch and Key shirts.

The transcontinental bargain hunter also hits Italy's Pratesi outlet (to plunk down lira on bed linens that cost hundreds of dollars per sheet in stateside stores); the January department store sales at Harrods and Harvey Nichols in London; and the tailors' shops in Hong Kong and Bangkok, where copies of designer clothing are custom-made for a fraction of the price of the real thing. The sophisticated shopper who considers a status look more important than authenticity (and legality) will even fly to Korea to hit the counterfeit designer marts in Seoul, where almost perfect copies of Mark Cross, Chanel, and Louis Vuitton handbags and suitcases sell for as little as twenty-five dollars in U.S. currency.

~

The *ultimate* sophisticated shopper is a mixture of all the above: someone whose wardrobe includes items from various countries, different labels, in all price ranges. Sophisticates mix and match designer with down-market—a Gap shirt with a Ralph Lauren suit, a DKNY sweater and Lee jeans, Giorgio Armani socks with Doc Martens shoes. After all, the object isn't to spend tons of money—it's to *look* as if you spent tons of money.

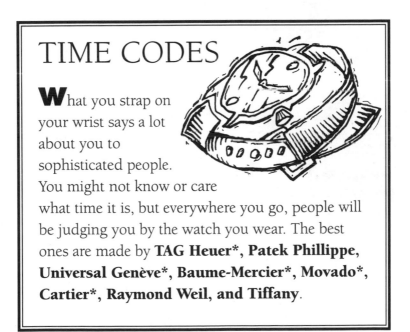

TIME CODES

What you strap on your wrist says a lot about you to sophisticated people. You might not know or care what time it is, but everywhere you go, people will be judging you by the watch you wear. The best ones are made by **TAG Heuer*, Patek Phillippe, Universal Genève*, Baume-Mercier*, Movado*, Cartier*, Raymond Weil, and Tiffany**.

Keep Up with the Trends

Even if you hate to shop, buying the "right" clothes isn't as hard as you might think. First, you must keep abreast of the fashion press—*Details* and *GQ* for men, *W* and *Harper's Bazaar* for women are good places to start. Next, get the catalogues for the more sophisticated mail-order houses and department stores that sell through the mail: Tweeds, Victoria's Secret, Bergdorf Goodman, Saks Fifth Avenue, Neiman-Marcus, Brooks Brothers, J. Peterman, the Horchow Collection, Arche shoes, etc. Now you're ready to start training yourself to choose less expensive versions of the most expensive fashions. You can order from the catalogues or brave the department stores and boutiques. And, if you think you just don't have good taste or an eye for fash-

HARDLY SOPHISTICATED

Please note: Unless you're a celebrity who owns a piece of one of the restaurants, wearing anything bearing the Hard Rock or Planet Hollywood logo just isn't done. Period. Acceptable T-shirts are those promoting rock tours or albums, souvenirs of a "cool" place (Maui, Taos, Key West), and those that are sports-related, especially if they're from a triathlon or marathon. That's it.

ion, take advantage of the personal shoppers who will help you go from department to department at most major stores, at no fee whatsoever—well, except for the expensive items they talk you into buying!

Sophisticated Fibers

To be sophisticated, it's not just what you wear that's important—it's what it's made out of as well. Silk is just one of many natural fabrics caressing cultured skins. Cotton, in various weaves and textures, is another favorite. In fact, now that the price of cotton has reached a new high, this fabric not only is coveted for its ecological correctness, it's also respected for its price tag.

You can raise your sophistication quotient immediately if you start shopping both fabric and fashion. If you can't judge a material by sight or feel, just reach inside for the little cleaning instruction tag. It will tell you at a glance if the fabric deserves a place of honor next to the sophisticated new you.

Sophisticates wear silk, tissue linen, cotton (especially Pima and Sea Isle), denim, cotton chino, microfiber (even though it's a polyester), rayon, cashmere, merino, fake fur, angora, mohair, wool, Lycra, silk velvet, panné, viscose, Harris tweed, suede, or frankly plastic vinyl.

Sophisticates don't wear ramie, polyester, double knits, wool blends, washable silk, acrylic, linen blends, cotton/poly blends, nylon, denim blends, vinyl trying to look like leather, gauze, pinwale corduroy, or anything appliquéd.

Shopping Around the World

The sophisticated shopper always seems to know the best place to buy what. If you want to impress someone with a gift, or with your own purchases, here's what you'll be looking at:

Amsterdam	Diamonds ("Would you mind picking up a flawless five-carat stone for me while you're overseas?"), Delft porcelain
Athens	Skyrian pottery, olives, pistachios
Brussels	Neuhaus chocolates, Val St. Lambert crystal
Copenhagen	Georg Jensen silver, Bang and Olufsen stereo equipment
Dublin	Waterford crystal, tweeds, heavy sweaters
Edinburgh	Smoked salmon, shortbread, single malt Scotch whiskey
Florence	Leather goods, paper desk accessories and stationery, cameos
Hong Kong	Custom-made copies of designer originals, genuine designer clothing from around the world
Honolulu	Macadamia nuts, antique Aloha shirts
London	Liberty print fabrics and accessories, Fortnum and Mason teas and gourmet foods, Turnbull and Asser shirts, lingerie from Janet Reger, bone china, Swaine and Adeney umbrellas

SOPHISTICATED ACCESSORIES UNDER $500

As sophisticated mothers always teach their children, accessories make the outfit. They'll also establish your reputation, if you purchase the right ones. These twenty items will add a certain élan to anything you wear and will never go out of style.

1. Mont Blanc pen
2. Gucci water bottle holder
3. Louis Vuitton wallet or billfold
4. Hermès* necktie
5. Filofax
6. Prada* tote bag
7. Movado wristwatch
8. Tiffany & Co. sterling pillbox
9. Paul Smith socks
10. Chanel costume jewelry
11. Mandarina Duck briefcase
12. Robert Clergerie* shoes
13. Donna Karan bodysuit
14. Polo knit polo shirt
15. Fogal of Switzerland pantyhose
16. Alfred Dunhill cigar case
17. Paloma Picasso lipstick
18. N. Peal cashmere muffler
19. Gap white cotton shirt
20. Ray Ban sunglasses

Los Angeles	Herbal elixirs, Jody Maroni sausages
Madrid	Lladró porcelain, embroidered linens
Mexico City	Silver jewelry, pottery
Milan	Housewares, designer clothing
Munich	Loden woolen wear, cuckoo clocks
New York	F. A. O. Schwartz toys, Steuben glass, Tiffany and Cartier jewelry

Paris	Perfume, designer clothing and accessories, Fauchon gourmet foods
Santa Fe	Native American art, handmade jewelry, Southwest paintings
Stockholm	Rosenthal porcelain, Nordska crystal
Thailand	Silks, Buddhas
Tokyo	Parasols, knives, pearls
Venice	Murano glass, masks
Zurich	Music boxes, Fogal hosiery, wristwatches

America's Sophisticated (and Affordable) Jewelry Designers

Forget diamonds, rubies, and pearls. Today's sophisticate is more likely to be wearing starkly simple sterling, unadorned gold, or simply elegant costume jewels. Invest in a piece or two of real jewelry or jewelry from these contemporary stars, and you'll find out that what you're wearing is tantamount to a big button announcing, "I've got great taste." The best are **Robert Lee Morris, Angela Cummings, Elsa Peretti, Paloma Picasso, Ericson Beamon, Lisa Jenks,** and **Judith Lieber.**

The Greatest and Most Expensive Designers

Why should you know the names of designers with price tags somewhere in the stratosphere? For one thing, you never know when you might come across an out-of-this-world bargain with fashion cachet. Everyone seems to know someone who snagged a nearly new Italian blazer at a church thrift shop or a French frock marked down to fifty dollars in the back room at Loehmann's.

For another, if you're going to dress with the best, it doesn't hurt to familiarize yourself with their names and their designs.

Most important, in the sophisticated scheme of things, knowing the names of fashion's favorites is every bit as important as wearing their creations—perhaps more so. Those in the know might not expect you to show up at their parties in a $3,000 Armani suit. But get caught muttering, "Giorgio *Who*?" and you might not be invited to show up again.

GIORGIO ARMANI

The reigning star of men's and women's fashion, Armani is known for his sparse, elegant designs and beautiful fabrics. Everyone who's anyone wears an Armani suit to the Academy Awards—his men's tuxedos are a must. In Milan, he's not just a designer, he's the city's top celebrity.

GEOFFREY BEENE

This Southerner wins the title of America's Most Elegant Designer—it's no surprise that even friends refer to him as "Mr. Beene." Nancy Reagan is a loyal client. The fashion press loves his feminine, conservative, yet slightly daring costumes, especially his extravagant gowns.

BILL BLASS

The quintessential American designer, Bill Blass also is the quintessence of sophistication. This handsome, suave man designs clothes just right for the country club set—understated and tailored, with ruffles in just the right places. Clients include Nancy Reagan, Barbara Bush, and Nancy Kissinger.

JEAN PAUL GAULTIER

This Frenchman designs on the cutting edge, using lots of leather, studs, laces, and form-fitting fabrics. His signature scent is packaged in a *bustier*-shaped bottle.

HUBERT DE GIVENCHY

He was Audrey Hepburn's favorite designer; and Jacqueline Kennedy Onassis's closet was filled with his clothes. He remains a fashion mainstay in *couture*.

DONNA KARAN

The Brooklyn-born best friend of Barbra Streisand found fame combining blouse tops with bodysuit bottoms to create blouses that never came untucked. Her clothes are called "wearable" by admirers, who can wear her designer line, her DKNY bridge line, her athletic line, her shoes, and her hosiery, while carrying one of her handbags and using her skin care, makeup, and signature fragrance. Her men's line, while casually elegant, hasn't yet had the same success. Noted for silk, school-girlish dresses, beautifully cut jackets, and cashmere sweatsuits.

REI KAWAKUBO*

Her Comme des Garçons label is the ultra-hip choice for the rich and trendy. Conservative dressers simply shake their heads over the artfully ripped seams, inside-out hems, and bulky fabrics she prefers. Consumers covet her men's suits, especially the black ones.

CALVIN KLEIN

The 1978 billboards for his jeans—Brooke Shields admitting that nothing came between her and her Calvins—brought him fame and fortune. His fragrances, especially Obsession, are best sellers. His clothing ranges from *couture* to super-casual, all featuring long, lean lines and earth-toned colors. Should we forgive him for unleashing Marky Mark upon the world?

KARL LAGERFELD

Chanel's not what it used to be, thanks to Karl Lagerfeld's inventiveness. He not only redesigned the legendary Chanel suit, he also started manufacturing versions in denim and leather, often trimmed with fake fur.

Known for his ponytail and the fan he carries, the German-born Parisian has made Chanel fun again—but the prices remain sky high.

RALPH LAUREN

The Bronx-born Ralph Lifshitz was a necktie salesman before founding Polo. He's one of the few designers to succeed in menswear prior to coming out with a women's line. He's since gone on to housewares, bed linens, bath towels—the works. He is known for moderately priced clothes that look like old money.

ISSEY MIYAKE

The master of pleats, this Japanese star designer recently introduced a "low-priced" collection with pieces in the $325 range. One of the leaders of the Japanese movement toward designing clothes that are about form rather than content, his most affordable line, Issey Miyake Plantation, is also available stateside.

JEAN MUIR

The *grande dame* of British designers, she's considered a purist who cuts beautifully and uses only the finest fabrics. She could be a bigger star, but prefers creating small collections at very high prices.

OSCAR DE LA RENTA

Although de la Renta's ruffles are world famous, his vibrant, brightly colored evening gowns are his trademark.

De la Renta's client list is filled with French names, many of which belong to "women of a certain age."

YVES ST. LAURENT

The Algerian-born St. Laurent is the star of French fashion, although he is admittedly neurotic as well as brilliant. He became the chief designer for Dior when he was just twenty-one, then went on to open his own fashion house. His opulent Moroccan- and Russian-inspired collections are his best.

EMANUEL UNGARO

His rippled, ruffled, and brightly colored *couture* collection is only for the rich, but his very affordable Emanuel collection, featuring sarong skirts and softly draped suits, is popular in the United States.

VALENTINO

An elegant man who designs for the richest women in the world, Valentino loves jewel-tone colors and turns out clothes more suitable for charity events and opening nights than the office.

GIANNI VERSACE

Leather breastplates, chain mail, transparent gold lamé— nothing's too outrageous for this Italian, whose U.S. popularity has soared since glamorous women like Cindy Crawford and Ellen Barkin started wearing his clothes to the Oscars.

VIVIENNE WESTWOOD

The Peck's Bad Girl of fashion, this British designer is loved for her avant-garde sense of humor. Her clothes are expensive but too kinky for all except the young and svelte. Her shoes often feature the highest platforms ever to strut down a runway. She's inspired many more famous—and wealthier—young designers.

YOHJI YAMAMOTO

The Zen prince of expensive chic, Yamamoto is known for his adventurous designs and incredible hand-woven fabrics. Men flip for his simple shirts while women love his jackets, which have traditional Japanese roots. If you see someone wearing a Yohji, odds are the garment is black.

Put Your Best Foot Forward
The Sophisticate's Favorite Shoe Labels

These boots are made for more than walking—they're made to instantly telegraph your taste level to others. Sure, you can get by with Keds, Florsheim, Nikes, or Joyce footwear much of the time; but when you want to be a big fish in the social swim, consider that a maître d' at one of London's top restaurants tells friends he judges diners' worthiness not by what they order from the menu but by how they're shod.

Arche*	**Gucci**
Manolo Blahnik	**Chanel**
Robert Clergerie	**Kenneth Cole**
Cole-Haan	**DKNY**
Ferragamo*	**Maud Frizon***
Stephane Kélian*	**Anne Klein**
Calvin Klein	**Bruno Magli**
Doc Martens	**Na Na**
Prada	**Walter Steiger**
Ellen Tracy	**Stuart Weitzman**

The Sophisticated Smoker

While smoking in general is now frowned upon and no longer considered sophisticated, savoring cigars still gets the stamp of sophistication, with smokers ranging from President Bill Clinton to Arnold Schwarzenegger to David Letterman. A cigar is made out of whole tobacco leaves, and it has three parts: filler, binder, and wrapper. Premium cigars are all hand-rolled and noted for burning evenly, while cheaper cigars are machine-made from compressed pieces of tobacco (with less predictable results). Cigars have their own unique system of measurement: length by ring gage (which is cigar-speak for "diameter"). A five-by-fifty cigar is one with a five-inch length and a ring gage of fifty.

Havana cigars can still be purchased—abroad. The majority of cigars sold in the United States use Honduran tobacco. Premium blends include Davidoff, Don Diego, Hoyo de Monterrey*, Macanudo*, and Partagas*.

The Sophisticated Home

Does your domicile mark you as a sophisticate? It does if you can answer "true" to at least half of the following statements.

1. Those lamps in my house which *aren't* antiques come from Milano.
2. I sleep between cotton or linen sheets with a thread count of two hundred or higher per inch.
3. My bathroom accessories are ceramic.
4. My napkins are linen or cotton.
5. My wineglasses are lead crystal, antiques, or funky imports.
6. I have oversized art books on my coffee table.
7. My bath towels are oversized, and 100-percent non-velour cotton.
8. I do not have self-sticking clothing hooks anywhere they might be seen by guests.
9. Photographs of my friends and relatives are displayed in simple yet elegant contemporary or antique frames, protected by glass and not plastic.
10. If there is a bookcase in the public area of my home, it does not hold paperbacks.

11. I purchase kitchen items at Williams Sonoma or The Pottery Barn; my cookware comes from kitchen supply houses.
12. Somewhere in my house you will find a needlepoint pillow.

THE ARTICULATE SOPHISTICATE

Arche (ar-SHAY)
Azzedine Alaïa (AZZ-uh-deen uh-LIE-uh)
Baume-Mercier (bowm mare-see-AY)
Bottega Veneta (boe-TAY-gah VEH-neh-tuh)
Cartier (karr-TEE-ay)
Chanel (SHAH-nell)
couture (koo-TOOR)
Donna Karan (KAIR-eyn)
Ferragamo (fair-a-GOMM-oh)
Gucci (GOO-chee)
Hermés (AIR-mez)
Hoyo de Monterrey (OYO day mahn-tuh-RAY)
Isaac Mizrahi (mizh-RAH-hee)
Issey Miyake (ISS-ee mee-YAWK-ee)
Macanudo (mack-a-NOO-doh)
Manolo Blahnik (BLAH-nick)
Maud Frizon (free-ZAHN)
Milan* (mee-LAHN)
Moschino (moe-SKEE-noh)
Movado (mow-VAH-doe)
Partagas (PAR-tuh-gus)

Prada (PRAH-dah)
Rei Kawakubo (RAY kah-wah-KOO-boe)
Rifat Ozbek (REE-faht OZH-bek)
Robert Clergerie (CLAIR-zhair-ee)
Stephane Kélian (KAY-lee-ahn)
TAG (togg) Heuer (HOY-er)
Universal Genéve (zhuh-NEV)
Yohji (YO-zhee) Yamamoto

Chapter Two

THE Sophisticated Sipper

Yesterday, you thought "Gewürtztraminer" was what you said when somebody sneezed, but tomorrow you'll be able to pass as an oenophile* (wine expert). Just read on.

First things first. Wine is divided into two main groups—red and white. Yes, it *is* that simple. Of course, there's rosé, but try to buy a decent one in the United States. If you decide to sample rosé when in France or lazing by the pool in Martinique, just ask the waiter or *sommelier** (wine steward) for suggestions, sighing, "You know, the decent rosés just don't reach the States." The French love remarks like that.

For safety's sake, it's best to stick to three countries: California (trust us, Californians consider it a country), France, and Italy. German wines are almost impossible to fake knowledge of, much less pronounce. If, when dining out, someone suggests you choose a wine from

Deuschland, try smiling apologetically and saying, "To be perfectly honest, I prefer something with less *fruit.*"

Of the Spanish wines available stateside, stick to the simplest blancos and riojas and order only in Spanish restaurants. (*Rioja**, in addition to meaning "red," also is the name of a wine region in Spain, so it's easy to get a white wine when you thought you were ordering a red.)

Use California guidelines for Australia, where the climate and the grapes are much the same. As for other countries (and states) exporting wines—Portugal, Hungary, New York, Washington, Idaho, etc.—let's face it: what could you gain by passing yourself off as an expert?

Wine Basics

Before looking at our three geographical regions, let's take a quick look at general rules. First, you can't lose by sticking to the basic rule of red with meat and game, white with fish and fowl. Second, reds should be served at room temperature, even very lightly chilled (as from the cellar, *not* the fridge), while whites should be cool but not cold, since an icy wine loses the subtleties of flavor. Remember: Chill but don't kill.

The third rule is, don't bother trying to impress anyone by using "wine talk" about the "nose" or the "finish." Anyone who uses wine terms except at an official tasting is showing off. Better to act modest. The secret of bluffing is to keep it simple. So no wine snobbery, no ordering ancient and costly Bordeaux that requires decanting, no trying to outshine sommeliers. Ordering intelligently while acting modest will get you the respect you need.

This also holds true for tasting. Don't bother trying to act like a professional taster. Instead of making a big deal about sniffing the cork, simply swirl the tasting portion of wine in your glass (this better enables you to smell the wine), then take a sip.

What about vintages? If you're currently cribbing with one of those credit-card-sized vintage lists that purports to tell you "good" and "bad" years of various wines, ditch it. There are too many variations from one vineyard to the next to lump them all together. Just take the plunge. And if you happen to wind up with a real woofer—say, a 1983 Bull Terrier Hills Merlot—just sigh disappointedly and murmur, "What a shame. The '82 was delicious!"

California Wines

California has about nine trillion wineries, so no one's heard of all of them. Look for wines from vineyards in Napa, Sonoma, Santa Barbara, Carneros and Monterey—popular wine areas—and plan to spend $14 to $28 for a good bottle of white wine in a restaurant (half that in a store, since the usual markup is 100 percent); $18 to $34 for red.

The California Cellar

Name	Pronunciation	Color	Comments
Zinfandel	ZIN-fan-dell	Red	Light and spicy. A "casual" rather than "serious" wine.
White Zinfandel	See above	Blush	The big kids' Shirley Temple. Not a sophisticate's first choice.
Merlot	mare-LOW	Red	A rich wine sophisticates love. Heavy enough for red meat, light enough for poultry.
Chardonnay	shar-dun-AY	White	Tends to have an "oaky" taste due to fermentation in oak barrels. Very dry.
Sauvignon Blanc	saw-veen-YAWN blonk	White	A light white wine with a lightly herbaceous or "grassy" taste. Dry, but less dry than Chardonnay.
Fumé Blanc	FOO-may blonk	White	Same as Sauvignon Blanc.
Cabernet Sauvignon	CAB-ber-nay saw-veen-YAWN	Red	A full-bodied red considered one of California's great successes. Terrific with red meat.
Pinot Noir	PEE-no nwaar	Red	Similar to Cabernet Sauvignon.
Chenin Blanc	shay-NAN blonk	White	Fruity. Ranges from semi-sweet to semi-dry.
Petite Sirah	peh-TEET see-RAH	Red	Deep. Purplish-red, somewhat astringent wine.

Italian Wines

Italy is a small country with a whole lot of wine, and the best of it has finally reached U.S. shores. The most renowned red wines—Barolo, Brunello di Montalcino*, Amarone*, Gattinara*—are considered every bit the equal of the best France has to offer. Stick to the mid-range ($24 to $40) with these wines, and you should do fine. For an even more affordable red wine, order a Chianti* or a Dolcetto*. In the past, when only Italy's most heavily produced wines reached this country, the word "Chianti" was usually associated with a heavy, grapey brew in a raffia-swathed bottle. Today's Chiantis are more refined, and often even superb. Italian white wines are as delicious as they are reasonably priced. You'll rarely go wrong with a Gavi or Pinot Grigio*. Expect to pay from $14 to $28 in a restaurant for a light, dry, tasteful bottle.

Italian Wine Laws

For close to thirty years, the Italian government has had wine laws known as *Denominazione di Origine Controllata,* or DOC. There are currently more than two hundred DOC regions, or zones, and a DOC wine must be produced within a specified region. Thus, the DOC appellation on a wine is widely considered a symbol of quality.

Wine from grapes grown within an inner DOC zone may be labeled *classico*. This could be considered a step up on the superiority ladder.

ITALIAN WINE TERMS

Italian	English
bianco*	white
dolce*	sweet
frizzante*	lightly sparkling
rosato*	rosé
rosso*	red
secco*	dry
spumante*	sparkling

The most select category is DOCG, or *Denominazione di Origine Controllata e Garantiti*.

Not all wines qualify for any of these labels and those bearing a DOC, classico, or DOCG marking are bound to be more expensive but also are your most dependable buys.

A relatively new category is IGT, or *Indicazioni Geografiche Tipiche*. These wines are considered of better quality than a lowly *vino da tavola* (table wine, which can still be extremely good).

French Wines

Wines from Burgundy are those in bottles with sloped sides, while those from Bordeaux arrive in square-shouldered bottles. People spend years learning how to buy *les vins de France*, so you'll want to tread very gingerly here, which you can do by sticking to the mid-priced Burgundies, both red and white. Beaujolais, a hearty red wine, is a safe red bet, as is the more complex Côtes du Rhône. The Bordeaux from the Médoc district are known for their sophistication and finesse; prices range from moderate to astronomical, and you'll find the most affordable if you look for those from Saint-Estèphe and Saint-Julien.

Dependable white Burgundies include those from the Loire Valley (Sancerre, Muscadet, and Vouvray), which are as crisp and grassy as the California Sauvignon Blancs. Don't overlook wines from the Mâcon area—Pouilly Fuissé, Saint-Véran, and Mâcon Blanc being the most readily available in the States.

French Wine Laws

The French wine laws, or *Appellation Contrôlée**, were established sixty years ago to guarantee that the wine in the bottle was from the place named on the label. As in Italy, there are more than two hundred zones.

The *Appellation Contrôlée* can be an entire region, a smaller district, an even smaller village, or even a single vineyard. These are considered France's best wines, and the words *Appellation Contrôlée* are clearly marked on the label. These wines—such as Bordeaux, Côtes du Rhône*, Montrachet*, Graves—offer the top wine selections.

Wines from Bordeaux (called "claret" in England) are usually further identified on their labels by the word *château*. Though this is the French word for "castle," on wine labels it usually means simply a specific vineyard (on the grounds of which one can expect to find a house rather than a palatial dwelling).

The next step down on the wine scale are the *Vins de Pays*, followed by plain old *vin ordinaire*. Vin ordinaire, as anyone who has ever quaffed liters of the local wine in Provence or the Loire Valley will attest, can be far from ordinary and should be tasted.

Beaujolais *Nouveau* for the *Nouveau* Sophisticate

The late fall in England and the United States is usually marked by the arrival of signs in front of pubs and liquor stores announcing, "The Beaujolais *nouveau** has arrived!" The non-sophisticate's normal reaction might be to inquire, "Isn't older supposed to be better?"

Beaujolais *nouveau,* or "new Beaujolais," is a special case. Referring to wines bottled and consumed within weeks of the harvest, these are wonderful drinks for those who prefer their red wine light and delicate.

The wine sophisticate can become fanatical about the Beaujolais *nouveau*, not only because of the wine's fresh, lively flavor, but also because of its scarcity. Don't look for these wines any time other than in November and December, as their life is limited and their sales brisk. Happily, their price is cheap. Beaujolais *nouveau* is best served cool. A half-hour in the fridge before serving will suffice.

Sparkling Facts about Champagne—France

When it comes to real celebrations, it's time to pop the cork on the champagne. Though there are many sparkling wines, the only true champagne is that from the Champagne region of France, not far from Paris.

French champagnes are the priciest and most admired. A champagne labeled Blanc de Blancs is one made from only white Chardonnay grapes. These light, delicate wines are considered the top champagnes by many connoisseurs. A champagne labeled Blanc de Noirs has been made entirely from black grapes such as Pinot Noir, and tends to be correspondingly richer in flavor.

French champagnes are categorized by the amount of sugar added just before the bottles are corked: demi-sec is the sweetest, dry or sec is still quite sweet, extra dry or extra sec is drier, and brut is the driest of all. While *brut* is the favorite of most champagne drinkers (the less sweetening added, the better the wine must be, since there is less sugar to mask poor quality), a somewhat sweeter champagne is advised for serving with dessert.

Most champagne seen in the U.S. is sold by the bottle. Occasionally a magnum (which holds two bottles) is spied. Rarely does one see splits (quarter bottles); though half-bottles are quite popular. As for the older, larger bottles—the jereboams (four bottles), rehoboams (six bottles), and methuselahs (eight bottles)—these appear most often in champagne lovers' dreams.

Sparkling French wines not produced in Champagne are know as *mousseux**.

Champagne labels that get attention include: Dom Perignon, Louis Roederer, Laurent Perrier, Perrier-Jouet, Taittinger*, Bollinger, and Veuve Clicquot*.

Sparkling Facts about Champagne— Other Countries

Italy's sparkling wines, called *spumantes*, come in all varieties—red, white, dry, sweet. The most well-known, Asti Spumante, is a sweet wine best relegated to the dessert course. Drier wines, prepared according to the same *méthode champenoise* that produces champagne in France, are categorized as *metodo classico* in Italy.

German sparkling wines are called *Sekt*, and are invariably fruity and sometimes quite sweet.

Spanish sparkling wines, known as *espumosos**, are dry, inexpensive, and extremely popular in the United States.

In the United States, the sparkling wines are called "champagne." The French, so strict about the use of that word, are less than thrilled—though that hasn't kept many of the large French firms from starting their own U.S. vineyards and labels. The two words most often heard in connection with sparkling wines from New York State are "Forget it!" Those from the West Coast are strongly recommended by many wine experts.

Seven Sophisticated Cocktails

BLACK RUSSIAN

Fill a rocks glass with ice. Add 1½ ounces of Vodka, top with ¾ ounce Kahlua, then serve with a stirrer. (For a White Russian, shake the ingredients along with 1 to 1½ ounces of milk or cream.)

BLOODY MARY

Pour 1½ ounces of vodka into a tall glass filled with ice. Fill the glass ¾ full with tomato juice, then add the juice of half a lemon, a dash of both Worcestershire sauce and Tabasco, ½ to 1 teaspoon horseradish, and salt and pepper. Stir vigorously, or put a cocktail shaker over the top of the glass and shake. Serve with a wedge of lime.

GIMLET*

Shake one ounce of gin or vodka with one ounce of Rose's lime juice. Serve straight up in a martini glass or on the rocks.

KIR*

Fill a white wine glass ¾ full with a dry white wine, then add one teaspoon crème de cassis (currant liqueur). Stir gently.

MARTINI

Fill a cocktail shaker with ice. Add gin (or vodka) and dry vermouth in a ratio of 5:1 or 7:1. Gently stir. Serve on the rocks or straight up with a cocktail olive (pitted, no pimiento) or a lemon twist. (Or drop in a pearl onion and call it a Gibson.)

MARGARITA

Shake together with ice 1½ ounces of tequila, ½ ounce of Cointreau or triple sec, and the juice of half a lime. Run a cut lemon around the rim of a large cocktail glass, then rim the glass with salt before filling it with the liquid. (This drink also can be served on the rocks or blended with ice.)

STINGER

Shake or stir 1 ounce of brandy with 1 (or ½ for a drier drink) ounce of white crème de menthe. Serve straight up or on the rocks.

The Sophisticated New After-Dinner Drink: Grappa

Okay, so it tastes like diesel fuel. Grappa* is still the chic after-dinner libation these days. An Italian brandy made from wine must (mashed grapes), stems, and pips after the juice has been crushed from them, grappa isn't new—Ernest Hemingway drank it (amongst many other alcoholic beverages)—but it is newly appreciated in the United States. The reason for its new-found popularity? Chalk it up to the high prices that spell luxury to sophisticates. Grappa, which should be sipped after dinner like cognac, can cost hundreds of dollars a bottle. And the most expensive grappas often come in thin-necked, blown-glass bottles that are works of art in themselves. It's an acquired taste, and the acquisition doesn't come cheap. But you can prove your sophisticate's credentials by ordering a glass in an upscale or Italian restaurant.

H$_2$0 Hot List

Once upon a time, people thought one of the great things about water was that it was free. Not any more. Designer water—both still and sparkling—is *de rigueur* these days, especially with the sophisti-sips. Europeans have always preferred their water bottled, believing the mineral content of water from natural underground springs has health benefits. Now Americans have followed their lead: In addition to seven hundred native brands, there are also more than seventy-five imports. Here are a few you might happen upon.

PERRIER*

This French water sparkles inside its cool green bottle.

EVIAN*

The best-selling water in the world is a still water, dates back to 1789, and comes from the French Alps. Evian also is sold in an aerosol can for skin care.

VOLVIC*

You can buy this French volcanic spring water with a low mineral content in movie theaters in U.S. cities.

NAYA*

This Canadian water is named after a goddess.

SAN PELLIGRINO*

A fizzy (*con gaz*) water from Italy.

POLAND SPRING

Faithful old American water from Maine. It won the Medal of Excellence at the 1893 Chicago World Exposition.

OZARKA

Yup, even Texas has its own designer quencher.

Microbrewery Mania

Today's sophisticated sipper wants the best, and that doesn't necessarily mean cracking a can of old, familiar brew. As beer becomes more and more an urbane beverage of choice, the number of

"UNA BIRRA, PER FAVORE!" - Beers Around The World

Ordering an import beer will do more for your image that knocking back the Zima. Here are some available across the United States.

Asahi* - Japan	Molson* - Canada
Brassin de Grarde - France	Moosehead - Canada
Carta Blanca - Mexico	Moretti - Italy
Chimay Ale - Belgium	Newcastle Brown Ale - England
Dortmünder Union - Germany	Ngok* - Congo
Dos Equis* - Mexico	Perroni* - Italy
Dragon Stout - Jamaica	Pilsner Urquell - Czechoslovakia
Dubel* - Belgium	Pripps - Sweden
Edelweiss* - Austria	Red Stripe - Jamaica
Fischer - France	Ringness - Norway
Foster's - Australia	Samuel Smith - England
Grolsch* - Netherlands	San Miguel - Philippines
Harp - Ireland	Singha - Thailand
Heineken - Netherlands	St. Pauli Girl - Germany
Kingfisher - India	Tsingtao* - China
Kirin - Japan	Whitebread Ale - England
Kronenbourg* - France	Würzburger - Germany
Mackeson's Stout - England	

microbreweries—small, "boutique" concerns making beer and ale the old-fashioned way, often with unique formulas—grows as well.

Some of the best known include:

Anchor Brewing Company, San Francisco - Home of Anchor Steam Beer, one of the original boutique favorites

Blitz-Weinhard Company, Portland, Oregon - Brewers of Henry Weinhard's Private Reserve and other beers

Samuel Adams, Boston - Known for Scottish-style ales

Devil Mountain Brewery, Benicia, California

Dixie, New Orleans

Wynkoop Brewing Company, Denver

Portland Brewing, Portland, Oregon - Love that Honey Beer!

Redhook Brewery, Seattle

Celis Brewery, Incorporated, Austin, Texas - Celis White Hill Country Beer turns cloudy when chilled.

Wasatch Brewing Company, Salt Lake City - Their Raspberry Wheat brew actually uses fresh fruit.

Jet City, Seattle - Their Rocket Red is a hot commodity.

Boutique Bourbon and Single Malt Scotch

Hard liquor is making a comeback in the sophisticated marketplace, and scotch and bourbon are now so popular that many chic eateries and bars have special whiskey menus.

Single malt scotch is nothing new. What *is* new are the number of imbibers who have discovered Scotland's proud distillations. They are known for their more-refined, woody flavors. The most famous in the United States are Glenfiddich, Glenlivet, The Macallan, and Laphroaig*. Most distilleries offer a variety of single malt scotches under their label, with different aging processes and time periods.

Boutique bourbons—also known as "small batch" or "barrel" bourbons—are a recent development that resulted from distilleries refining brands for the Asian market by allowing the barrels to age longer. The richer product rapidly caught on with hip young Americans, who previously had made Jack Daniels their bourbon of choice.

The best-known boutique bourbon is Maker's Mark, which is distilled in Louisville, Kentucky, in the only beverage facility that's a national historic landmark. In the last few years, Maker's Mark has established itself as the sophisticate's choice.

The larger distilleries have come out with their own small batch bourbons. These include: Bookers, Bakers, and Nob Creek (from Jim Beam Company); and Blantons, Rock Hill, and Elmer Lee (from Ancient Age Distillery).

Purists still call for Maker's Mark, since it flows from a single-line distillery, rather than from a large distillery bottling under several different brand names.

How Do You Spell "Cognac"? C-L-A-S-S

By definition, cognac is a wine brandy made only from grapes grown in the French district of Charentes, near the town of Cognac. All cognac is brandy—however, only the finest brandy is cognac.

Look for stars (e.g., ☆☆☆☆), on the bottle, which are ratings of the contents, as well as the letters "VSOP" (Very Superior Old Pale) or X.O. (extra old). Top brands include Rèmy Martin, Martell, Hennessy, Hine, and Courvoisier*.

Armagnac* is a close relative of cognac. It also comes from the southwestern area of France and is made with the same grape. However, because it's aged differently, the taste is drier and more pungent than cognac. Armagnac has surpassed cognac as the after-dinner libation of choice for the severely sophisticated (that is, except for those with the fortitude to drink grappa).

The Sophisticate's Guide to Glassware

Red Wine Glass Stem glass with a rounded bowl (*red wine*)

White Wine Glass Stem glass with a straight, rather narrow bowl (*white wine, kir*)

All-Purpose Wine Glass Stem glass with a bowl more rounded than a white wine glass and less rounded than a red wine glass. This is the type of stemware used at tastings (*red or white wine*)

Brandy Snifter A short-stemmed glass with a bowl wide at the bottom, tapering toward the top—the better to warm and savor the aroma of the contents (*cognac, armagnac*)

Liqueur Glass — A short-stemmed, very narrow glass (*liqueurs, grappa*)

Sherry Glass — Small stem glass with a bowl narrow at the bottom and widening at the top in a trumpet shape (*sherry*)

Martini Glass — Stem glass with a shallow bowl that spreads from the stem at about a 120-degree angle (*martini, Manhattan, gimlet, other clear cocktails served "straight up"*)

Old-Fashioned Glass — Medium-sized, wide glass with straight or very slightly sloping sides (*old-fashioned, Bloody Mary*)

Rocks Glass — Smaller version of an old-fashioned glass (*straight whiskey with ice, Black Russian, rusty nail*)

Whiskey Sour Glass — Slightly narrower and shorter version of a white wine glass (*whiskey sour, assorted cocktails*)

Tom Collins Glass — Straight-sided tumbler (*Tom Collins, Bloody Mary with ice, other "tall" drinks*)

Cocktail Glass — A wide, shallow stem glass (*margarita, daiquiri, other blended cocktails*)

Champagne Glass — A stem glass with a long, narrow bowl, also called a "champagne flute" (*NOTE: the stem glass with a wide, very shallow bowl often used for champagne is not a sophisticated choice, as this glass lets the champagne bubbles escape too quickly.*)

Beer Glass — A narrow tumbler with sides that slope and widen at the mouth of the glass (*beer*)

THE ARTICULATE SOPHISTICATE

Amarone (am-ah-ROE-neh)
Appellation Contrôlée (ap-pel-LAY-shun kon-troe-LAY)
Armagnac (AR-men-yak)
Asahi (uh-SAH-hee)
Beaujolais (boe-zhoe-LAY) nouveau (noo-VOE)
bianco (bee-AHN-koh)
Brunello di Montalcino (mawn-tah-CHEE-noh)
Chianti (key-AHN-tee)
Côtes du Rhône (cote doo RONE)
Courvoisier (koor-vwah-see-AY)
Dolcetto (dol-CHETT-oh)
dolce (DOHL-chee)
Dos Equis (dohs ECK-ees)
Dubel (doo-BELL)
Edelweiss (AID-el-vice)
espumoso (ess-poo-MOE-so)
Evian (EH-vee-ahn)
frizzante (frizz-AHN-tay)
Gattinara (gatt-ee-NAH-rah)
Gimlet (GIM-let)
Grappa (GROP-pa)
Grolsch (GROHLSH)
Kir (KEER)
Kronenbourg (KROW-nen-berg)
Laphroaig (la-FROIG)
Montrachet (mawn-truh-SHAY)
Molson (MOHL-sun)
mousseux (moo-SEW)
Naya (NIGH-ya)

Ngok (NOCK)
oenophile (EEN-uh-file)
Perrier Jouet (pair-ee-AY joo-AY)
Perroni (pair-OWN-ee)
Pinot Grigio (PEE-noh GREE-zhee-oh)
Rioja (ree-OH-ha)
rosato (roe-ZAHT-toe)
rosso (ROE-so)
San Pelligrino (san pehl-i-GREEN-oh)
secco (SEK-o)
sommelier (sum-uhl-YAY)
spumante (spoo-MAHN-tay)
Taittinger (TAT-en-zhoy)
Tsingtao (sing-DOW)
Veuve Clicquot (vuuv klee-KOE)
Volvic (VAUL-vick)

Chapter Three

Gourmet

The sophisticated gourmet lives to eat quality, not quantity. Dining preferences are, in fact, one of the most common tests of one's sophistication quotient. Someone who thinks sweetbreads are a dessert, shies away from the sushi bar, or considers chow mein the peak of Chinese cuisine can be embarrassed easily when dining amongst the elite. The other reason for studying the grazing habits of the urbane is even simpler: If you know a *rognon** from an *entrecôte**, you won't find yourself staring down a kidney when you were expecting a nice juicy steak.

An appreciation of food from many countries is the mark of the truly sophisticated palate. Be prepared to sample native dishes from Morocco to Malaysia if you'll be dining with a worldly crowd. And, because the amount of red meat eaten tends to decline with the level of sophistication attained, expect more fish and chicken if you're climbing the social ladder. Real men may eat slabs o' beef, but real sophisticates prefer rare ahi* tuna. The good news for the squeamish is that the craze for the "new American cuisine" (as opposed to *nouvelle* * cuisine, which combines strange bedfellows on the order of duckling with red cabbage and kiwi fruit) means such standards as meat loaf and mashed potatoes are enjoying a new vogue.

French Food

These are *not* French foods: French fries, French toast, French's mustard. It's easy to get confused, since no one's absolutely sure anymore exactly what French food *is*.

At one point, every sophisticate had this down pat. French food was steak and *pommes frites* *, their version of fries, much skinnier than those usually seen in the U.S. French food was heavy sauces, with heart-clogging dollops of heavy cream. French food was lamb with white beans, chicken drenched in wine, and seafood oozing butter.

Then along came France's *nouvelle cuisine*, or the "new food," which has practically overshadowed traditional French cooking. Lighter, more calorie-conscious fare featuring unique combinations such as chicken breasts with raspberries and vinegar, *nouvelle cuisine* became a very big deal—well, almost a war, as France split into traditionalists and adventurers over every meal.

Today, in the States and abroad, the name of a restaurant won't tell you what kind of French food you're getting. If you want the hearty, stick-to-the-ribs-and-arteries food France got known for in the first place, inquire if the restaurant serves "classic" cuisine.

The Five Rules of Caviar

1 Serve with a glass, plastic, or mother-of-pearl spoon. Never serve with a metal implement, which spoils the taste.

2 Don't dump caviar in a bowl (unless you own a special caviar server). Open the glass jar or tin and set it in a bowl of crushed ice.

3 If you serve caviar as an hors d'oeuvre, serve non-salty snacks alongside to balance the saltiness of the roe.

4 Never freeze or cook caviar. If using caviar in cooking, add the roe to the food after it's been cooked.

5 Don't serve sweet or strongly flavored drinks with caviar. A dry champagne or an ice-cold vodka are the suggested beverages.

The Ultimate French Food

There are certain accompaniments the French consider a necessity when dining. First is wine, for digestive purposes and the pure pleasure of life. Second is bread. The French prefer the long, thin bread properly called a *baguette**. Third is cheese—and hang the cholesterol! Popular French cheeses include Brie*, St. André* and other rich triple crème cheeses, Camembert*, and Montrachet, a crumbly goat cheese. Cheese is served before dessert and after salad in classic French dining. The salad is presented *after* the main course. The fourth necessity at the French table is strong coffee, often accompanied by liqueurs, after dinner.

Something Fishy: Caviar

Almost as precious as gold, caviar, which sells for about sixty dollars an ounce, is considered the food of the gods by many in possession of sophisticated palates. To others, fish eggs are fish eggs, no matter what they're called, and the fuss about this "black gold" is puzzling.

Though the name is now applied to a variety of fish roe much less expensive, the name "caviar" should rightfully be reserved for the tiny, deep-gray eggs of the sturgeon. Rare and coveted, they are the ideal cosmopolitan snack when served with ice-cold vodka and champagne

MUSHROOMS: FOOD FOR THE GODS

It was the ancient Greeks who decided these tasty fungi were created for the immortals. Today, the sophisticates have rediscovered the magic of mushrooms. The more obscure the variety, the better.

Porcini*	Dried then imported from Italy, these nutty-flavored mushrooms are great in dishes featuring game or poultry.
Portobello*	Known as "the poor man's steak," this mushroom is thick and meaty and often served grilled. The latest "in" food in chic restaurants now that so many are shunning meat is the Portobello Burger, featuring a thick, grilled mushroom in place of a meat patty.
Shiitake*	Popular in sauces and Asian cooking, this mushroom has a deep and woodsy flavor.
Morel*	The penny pincher's truffle, this delicate morsel is imported in dried form from Europe, soaked, then sautéed before being added to sauces.
Oyster Mushroom	This delicate, sweet, white mushroom is often seen in Asian dishes.
Chanterelle*	This trumpet-shaped, pale-gold mushroom hails from France and tastes slightly fruity.

and a plate of blinis* (thin crêpes) in the Russian manner, unbuttered toast points, or dry rusks.

Russia and Iran are the countries long associated with caviar, though tasty, less expensive varieties are now being distributed from China and the United States. The smaller quantities and roes of lower quality are usually sold in glass jars, while the really *primo* caviar comes in tins. The gourmet's delight is the kilogram (2.2. pounds) tin.

Malossal refers to premium roe, the *crème de la crème*, noted for its deep, pearly gray color.

The taste is salty, the cholesterol count is alarming, the overall experience unique. If you've never tried caviar, do start with the real thing, rather than a cheaper roe. To look like a true aficionado, skip the chopped egg white and yolk and onions often served as an accompaniment and squeeze just a drop of fresh lemon onto those precious baubles.

And, whatever you do, don't cook the eggs!

Types of caviar you might come across include:

LUMPFISH Various tiny black eggs often substituted for caviar, lumpfish is cheap but shouldn't be scorned. It's saltier and fishier, but it can be delicious and is easily found in supermarkets and even liquor stores.

WHITEFISH Mildly flavored, this kosher caviar features tiny eggs and is often sold in delicatessens.

BELUGA*	From the Beluga sturgeon, this roe is the most expensive, with the mildest, least salty flavor. Each egg is approximately half the size of a pea.
SEVRUGA*	Still costly, these eggs are smaller and slightly saltier than Beluga. They are considered the best buy in terms of cost and flavor. Still, you *could* buy an entire dinner—or two—for the price of a wee ounce.
OSETRA*	These golden-brown eggs are only slightly larger than sesame seeds. They add an especially artistic touch when nestling next to Beluga or Sevruga.
"PRESSED" CAVIAR	This paste-like blend of crushed and imperfect sturgeon eggs is the poor man's caviar, scorned by true gourmets.
AMERICAN	These small silver-gray eggs come from the paddlefish and are similar to Sevruga, though saltier, and considerably lower in price.
SALMON	Coral eggs the size of small peas, this roe is inexpensive and often seen as a garnish or in sushi.

Always Order the Chicken

When in doubt, they say, go for the fowl.

Murghi Korma, India
MURR-ghee ("g" as in "get") CORE-ma
Mild chicken curry with yogurt

Tandoori Murgh, India
tan-DOO-ree MURG
Akin to barbecued chicken; roasted with spices in a tandoor (clay oven)

B'stilla or Bestilla, Morocco
bess-TEE-ya
Minced chicken with ground almonds and cinnamon in phyllo dough. Yummy.

Saté Ayam, Indonesia
sat-TAY EYE-yom
Spicy grilled chicken on skewers

Kai Yang (or Gai Yang), Thailand
KIGH yahng
Garlic Chicken

Pad Thai, Thailand
PADD tie
Noodles with chopped peanuts, pork, chicken, and shrimp

Tori Teriyaki, Japan
TOE-ri tear-ree-YOCK-ee
Chicken grilled with a sweet marinade

Goma Yaki, Japan
GO-mah YOCK-ee
Fried chicken sprinkled with sesame seeds

Adobobong Manok, Philippines
ah-DOH-bahng ma-NOKE
Chicken stewed with spices then fried and served with hot
coconut milk sauce

Dak Jim, Korea
dahk ZHEEM
Stewed chicken served with rice and kim chi (or kimchee),
spicy pickled cabbage

Kung Pao Gee Ding, China
kung pow JEE ding
Spicy chicken with peanuts

Bo Lo Gee, China
bow low JEE
Sweet and sour chicken with pineapple

Coq au vin, France
COKE oh vhen
Chicken simmered in red wine sauce with mushrooms and onions

Poulet rôti, France
poo-LAY row-TEE
Roast chicken

Pollo con porcini, Italy
POHL-lo cone por-CHEE-nee
Chicken with mushrooms

Pollo alla griglia, Italy
POHL-lo AH-lah GREE-lyah
Grilled chicken

Arroz con pollo, Spain
ah-ROSE cone POLE-yo
Chicken with rice

By the way, caviar as an emblem of sophistication is nothing new. "The play, I remember, pleased not the million; 'twas caviare [sic] to the general," noted Shakespeare in *Hamlet*.

Italian Food

The most popular foreign cuisine, now found almost everywhere throughout America, is Italian. There are, in fact, many regional styles of Italian cooking (Tuscan, Neapolitan, etc.), but there are only two main divisions: Northern and Southern. Northern Italian food concentrates on meat and game. Risotto*, (a blend of rice, butter, broth, and anything from vegetables to seafood), also is popular; so are pastas. Tomato sauces aren't seen here often, except in the meaty sauces from Bologna. Southern Italy, on the other hand, serves red sauces and spicy foods. Red sauces with shellfish are a specialty. Genuine Italian pizza, unlike the American versions, has a very thin crust and little cheese or sauce.

An authentic Italian dinner consists of many courses, with pasta served between the appetizer and the main course. Lighter eaters, especially in the United States, often choose pasta as the main course.

Know Your Noodles

Everyone loves pasta, but once noodles go beyond the realm of spaghetti and linguine, even the most sanguine sophisticate can get confused. Italian chefs consider various shapes best for various dishes, usually due to the ability of their whorls and swirls to hold sauce. Use this pasta guide, and observe the cardinal rule when cooking *pastasciutta** or "pasta with sauce": Serve it *al dente**, which means firm to the teeth and never mushy.

AGNOLOTTI *ah-nyoh-LOHT-tee*
crescent-shaped ravioli with filling

BUCATINI *boo-kah-TEE-nee*
short, straight macaroni

CANNELLONI *kahn-nel-LOH-nee*
large tubes usually filled with ground meat, then topped with white sauce and browned in the oven

CAPELLI D'ANGELO *kop-PEHL-lee don-SJAY-loh*
"angel hair" pasta, the thinnest strands of all

CAPPELLETTI *kop-pehl-LET-tee*
similar to tortellini, these differ in shape—they are round (the name means "little hats") and are filled

CAVATELLI *kah-vah-TELL-ee*
short shells with a crinkled edge

CONCHIGLIE *kahn-KEE-glee-ah*
pasta shells

FARFALLE *far-FAL-leh*
bowtie pasta

FETTUCINE *feht-too-CHEE-nee*
fat, narrow ribbons

FUSILLI *foo-SEE-lee*
small spirals ("little springs")

LASAGNA *lah-SAH-nyah*
layers of broad noodles alternating with meat or vegetable sauce, béchamel sauce, and parmesan cheese

LINGUINE *leen-GWEE-nee*
thick but very narrow ribbons of pasta

MANICOTTI *mahn-nee-KOHT-tee*
giant tubes with filling

ORZO *OAR-zoh*
tiny, rice-shaped pasta

ORRECHIETTE *oh-reh-chee-EHT-ti*
small, ear-shaped pasta (the name means "little ears")

PAPPARDELLE *pah-par-DELL-leh*
broad noodles

PENNE *pehn-NAY*
small pasta tubes cut diagonally
at each end, like their name-
sake, "quills"

RAVIOLI *rah-VYOH-lee*
thin squares of pasta with filling

RIGATONI *ree-gah-TOE-nee*
macaroni-type pasta with large
tubes

ROTELLI *roh-TELL-lee*
small, wheel-shaped pasta

TAGLIATELLE *tah-lyah-TEHL-leh*
egg noodles similar to fettucine

TORTELLINI *tor-tehl-LEE-nee*
small stuffed pasta rings

TORTELLONI *tor-tehl-LOW-nee*
large stuffed pasta rings

VERMICELLI *vehr-mee-CHELL-lee*
very fine spaghetti

ZITI *ZEE-tee*
large curved tubes

Ten Signs You're Dining in a Sophisticated Restaurant

1 Salad dressings will never be listed on the menu as having been made with oil and vinegar. Instead, you can expect to see such ingredients as hazelnut or walnut oil, balsamic vinegar (an Italian wine vinegar aged in wood for a decade), and raspberry vinegar.

2 Table linens are fabric, never paper.

3 Vegetables are miniature (baby squashes and eggplants), served grilled, or both; potatoes are Technicolor (Yukon Gold, purple Fingerling).

4 The female servers wear the same uniforms as the males, and they're more likely to have been designed by Armani than to feature hankies pinned to the bosom.

5 Seared ahi tuna is on the menu.

6 The server delivers the food to the correct people without asking who gets what.

7 Unusual greens—radicchio*, mâche*, arugula* frisée*—prevail, while iceberg lettuce is missing in action.

8 The dessert list includes a choice of exotic *sorbets** or *gelato**, such as kiwi, mango, passionfruit, blood orange, papaya.

9 Parker House rolls are shunned in favor of chewy Italian *focaccia**, pumpernickel-raisin rolls, blue corn muffins, olive-studded loaves, hazelnut whole-wheat bread, and the like.

10 Pastas come in various colors ands flavors, e.g., red chile fettucine, green spinach orrechiette, pale burgundy beet linguine, yellow lemon-pepper penne.

Dining Phonetically
A Guide to French and Italian Menus

The hot cuisines in sophisticated restaurants are French and Italian. Now you'll know what you're being served!

FRENCH

AUBERGINE *OH-bear-gheen*
Eggplant

BOUILLABAISSE *BOO-ya-bess*
Fish and shellfish stew

CANARD À L'ORANGE *ka-NARD ah loh-RAHNGE*
Duck with orange sauce

CHOUCROUTE *choo-KROOT*
Casserole of pork, sauerkraut,
and potatoes

COQUILLES SAINT-JACQUES *koh-KEEL san zhahk*
Scallops, usually in a cream
and cheese sauce

COURGETTE *koor-ZHET*
Zucchini

CROISSANT *crwa-SAUNT*
A rich, buttery crescent roll

ESCARGOT *ess-kahr-GOH*
Snail

FOIE DE VEAU *fwa deh VOE*
Calf's liver

LÉGUMES *lay-GOOM*
Vegetables

LES VIANDS *lay vee-OND*
Meat or meats

VICHYSSOISE *VISH-chee-swahs*
Chilled potato-leek soup

APRÉS DÎNER

While sophisticates don't necessarily shovel down the desserts, most don't consider a meal complete without coffee. That means coffee *after* dinner, by the way—never before, which is considered very middle-class.

Beverage	Origin	Notes
Cafe Americano (kah-FAY ah-mare-ee-KAH-no)	Italy	Watered-down espresso
Café au lait (kah-FAY oh LAY)	France	Strong coffee diluted with hot milk, usually sipped at breakfast in an oversized cup.
Café filtre (kah-FAY FEEL-treh)	France	Coffee brewed in traditional French manner, which consists of pouring boiling water into a glass carafe filled with ground dark-roasted coffee. After the coffee has steeped several minutes, a plunger in the top of the carafe is pushed down, trapping the grounds. Experts say this is the absolute best way to brew coffee.
Caffe Latte (kah-FAY lah-TAY)	Italy	Small amount of strong coffee with large amount of steamed milk. In Italy, this is considered a breakfast drink.
Caffee Macchiato (kah-FAY ma-chee-AH-toe)	Italy	Espresso with just a few drops of steamed milk.
Cappuccino (kap-poo-CHEE-no)	Italy	Espresso topped with steamed milk. Sometimes topped with cinnamon, nutmeg, or ground chocolate.
Espresso (es-PRESS-o) (not expresso)	Italy	Very strong coffee made by using steam pressure to force boiling water through finely ground coffee held in a diaphragm. Served in a tiny cup with a sugar cube and a twist of lemon on the saucer.
Greek Coffee	Greece	See Turkish coffee.
Latte Macchiato (LAH-tay ma-chee-AH-toe)	Italy	Warm milk with just a few drops of coffee.
Turkish Coffee	Turkey	Coffee ground into a very fine powder, with boiling water added. The drinker is actually drinking the ground coffee beans dissolved in water. **Warning:** Drink this as soon as possible after serving or it turns to mud. Usually drank laden with sugar.

ITALIAN

CARPACCIO *kar-PAHT-cho*
Thin slices of raw beef with oil, lemon, and parmesan cheese

FAGIOLI *fah-JOL-lee*
Beans

FUNGHI *FOON-ghee*
Mushrooms

GNOCCHI *NYO-chee*
Tiny potato dumplings

INSALATA CAPRESE *een-sah-LAH-tah kah-PRAY-seh*
Salad of sliced tomatoes and mozzarella cheese

INSALATA MISTA *een-sah-LAH-yah MEE-stah*
Mixed salad

MELANZANA *meh-lahn-ZAHN-nah*
Eggplant

PROSCIUTTO *pro-SHOOT-toe*
Thinly sliced Parma ham

SCALLOPINE *skah-low-PEE-neh*
A thin slice of meat

TIRAMISÚ *tee-rah-mee-SOO*
Sweet dessert made with cake, sweet mascarpone cheese, and cocoa and/or powdered espresso

VITELLO TONNATO *vee-TEHL-low Tohn-NAH-toe*
Sliced cold veal covered with a tuna-and-mayonnaise sauce

Sushi Savvy

The prospect of eating bits of raw fish in combination with damp rice and perhaps a bit of dried seaweed is a major turn-on to many sophisticates, but this concept can be hard to swallow for the rest of the world. Should you find yourself at a sushi bar, in jeopardy of tossing your cookies with that first bite of uncooked piscine creature, just relax. Use this handy chart to order cautiously. You can even get by without being embarrassed that a single bit of raw fish has not passed your lips!

SUSHI Various types of foods served in small bites in combination with vinegared rice and, sometimes, seaweed.

SASHIMI Small slices of raw fish without rice or seaweed served with shredded daikon radish.

WASABI The very hot green paste served with sushi. This is made from powdered horseradish, so be forewarned. A pearl-sized bit of wasabi is stirred into a small saucer of soy sauce into which the individual pieces of sushi and sashimi are then dipped. Small, thin slices of pickled ginger are another accompaniment.

AMAEBI* Sweet shrimp. These are served with the heads delivered separately and are recommended only for the strong of stomach.

ANAGO* Sea Eel. This is served cooked, one small strip on rice, bound with a bit of seaweed and topped with a sweet sauce. Tasty.

AWABI* Abalone.

CALIFORNIA ROLL Crabmeat or surimi (fake crab) and avocado, wrapped in rice and seaweed to form long roll, which is cut into pieces. A joke to the Japanese, this is extremely popular in the States, where it has led to other occidental variations such as the deli roll (lox and cream cheese rolled with rice and seaweed).

EBI* Cooked, shelled shrimp sushi.

The Fine Art of Eating with Chopsticks

The serious sophisticate always asks for chopsticks when eating Asian food (even in Thai restaurants, regardless that most Thais use knives and forks). If you haven't mastered the art of eating a meal with two tapered wooden spindles, don't give up. It's quite simple, and practice makes perfect.

Here's how: Place the lower chopstick beneath your thumb, holding it closer to the lower (more pointed) end. You want to hold this chopstick stationary in the groove where your thumb meets your hand. The lower end of this chopstick should be propped against your middle finger (either against the pad or against the first joint). You then place the other chopstick between the pads of your thumb and index finger. This is the chopstick that moves, as you spread it open and then close it to hold food, using a firm and steady pressure to bring it to your lips.

Don't practice with rice. Asians use their chopsticks to push rice into their mouths as they hold their bowls up next to them.

HAMACHI* — Yellowtail. A mild fish.

HIRAME* — Hake or Halibut. This sushi is usually topped with green onion and a sweet sauce called Ponzi.

HOTATEGAI* — Scallop.

IKURA* — Salmon Roe. These large orange eggs are often topped with a raw quail's egg. Not for cholesterol watchers.

KAPPA MAKKI* — Cucumber roll. A vegetarian favorite.

MAGURO* — Tuna. A very mild fish with a buttery texture and red color. Albacore tuna (when available) has a creamy texture and pink-gray color. Easy for beginners.

MIRUGAI* — Giant Clam.

SAKE* — Salmon.

TAKO* — Octopus. Think "Goodyear."

TEKKA MAKKI* — Tuna roll. Similar to Kappa Makki but with chopped raw tuna in place of cucumber. Because a makki roll contains only a small amount of raw fish, this is a good place to start if you've never eaten raw fish before.

TORO* — Fatty tuna. Preferred over maguro by the Japanese for its deeper flavor.

UNAGI* Fresh water eel. Similar to sea eel.

UNI* Sea Urchin. Does anyone *really* like uni?

VEGETABLE ROLL A long, sliced roll holding a combination which might include daikon radish sprouts, carrots, cucumber, avocado, green onion, or any other combination of raw vegetables. Comparable to a small salad rolled up with rice and seaweed.

By sticking to the **bold-faced selections**, supplemented by other finger foods that can be ordered at the sushi bar (for example, gyoza*, [pork dumplings], shu mai* [shrimp dumplings], tempura* [batter-fried] vegetables and/or shrimp, miso* [bean paste] soup), it's possible to consume an entire meal at the sushi bar without (1) being forced to eat hefty chunks of raw fish, and (2) losing your cool—or your lunch.

THE ARTICULATE SOPHISTICATE

ahi (AH-hee)
al dente (ahl DEN-teh)
Amaebi (ah-MY-bee)
Anago (ah-NAW-go)
arugula (ah-ROO-guh-luh)
Awabi (ah-WAB-ee)
baguette (bag-GET)
Beluga (beh-LOO-guh)
blinis (BLIN-eez)
Brie (bree)
Camembert (KAM-mem-bare)
chanterelle (shawn-TRELLE)
Ebi (AY-bee)
entrecôte (AHN-treh-coat)
focaccia (foh-KOT-chia)
frisée (free-SAY)
gelato (jeh-LAH-toe)
gyoza (gee-OH-zah)
Hamachi (ha-MAW-chee)
Hirame (heer-AW-mee)
Hotategai (HOE-taat-eh-guy)
Ikura (ee-KOOR-uh)
Kappa Makki (KA-pah ma-KEE)
mâche (mahsh)
Maguro (ma-GOOR-oh)
Mirugai (MEER-uh-guy)
miso (MEE-so)
morel (MAWR-ell)
nouvelle (NOO-vell)

Osetra (oh-SET-truh)
pastasciutta (pah-stah-SHOOT-tah)
pommes frites (pom FREET)
porcini (por-CHEE-nee)
portobello (por-toh-BELL-oh)
radicchio (rah-DEEK-ee-oh)
risotto (rih-SO-toe)
rognon (rawn-YOHN)
Sake or Saki (SOCK-ee)
Sevruga (seh-VROO-guh)
shiitake (shee-TOCK-ee)
shu mai (SHOE my)
sorbets (sore-BAYS)
St. André (san AWN-dray)
Tako (TAH-koe)
Tekka Makki (MAW-kee)
tempura (tem-POOR-ah)
Toro (Toe-roe)
Unagi (oo-NAW-gee)
Uni (OO-nee)

Chapter Four

Investor

Even if the only investment you can call your own is some loose change in a piggy bank, you'll need to learn some basic words to hold your head high when the talk turns to finance.

BEAR

A "bear" is someone who sells a stock on the assumption that it's going to fall. This is known as "selling short." Someone who's "bearish" isn't necessarily in a growling mood, just pessimistic about market prices. And a "bear market" means the prices are falling. Why "bear"? Because back in the days when men still shot bears and sold their skins, they made the deals for the fur *before* the bears were shot.

BULL

The opposite of a bear, a "bull" is someone who, believing the price of a stock, bond, currency, or commodity is about to rise, buys in the hopes of turning a profit. A bull doesn't sell short but is said to be "long" on stock. The "bullish" person isn't stubborn—he or she is optimistic about the market. If it's a "bull market," optimism is the proper spirit, as the prices are generally rising.

BLUE CHIP

Not taco chips made from Southwestern blue corn, but shares of common stock in any big, well-known company with a reputation for continually paying dividends. Blue chip stocks don't come cheap—you pay more than the yield would justify, because you're paying for security and owning part of a winner.

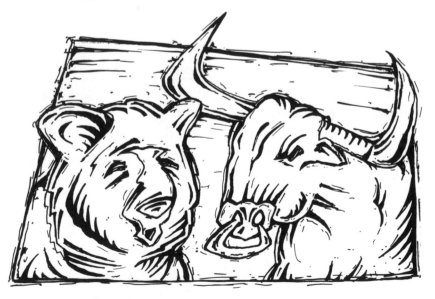

BOND

A long-term debt instrument, often issued by municipalities, which also is known as a fixed-income security because the bond owner receives regular payments at a fixed rate of interest. Formerly considered a safe, boring investment, bonds became riskier in the volatile market of the eighties.

DOW-JONES AVERAGE

Three groups of stock prices (representing thirty industrial companies, twenty transportation companies, and fifteen utilities) reported as three measures of the market's activity. The best-known is the industrial average, which is what the news is referring to when you hear, "The Dow is up ten points."

FANNIE MAE & GINNIE MAE

Nobody's maiden aunts, these terms stand for Federal National Mortgage Association and Government National Mortgage Association. When someone says they've bought Fannie or Ginnie Maes, they mean they've invested in lots of mortgages.

FED

When people mention "the Fed," they don't mean Dick Tracy. They're referring to the Federal Reserve System, the central bank of the United States, which consists of twelve individual banks around the country. The Fed is responsible for controlling the money supply.

Sophisticates and Money: Their Lips Are Sealed

While *having* money is considered a very sophisticated thing, *talking about it* is not. This is good news for the less-than-prosperous individual. If you look the part and act the part, no one's going to ask you how much you've got in the bank. And if they do, the sophisticated reaction is to answer vaguely, without giving any hint of your financial status. "I'm rolling in it" or "I pull in 120 K a year" are not proper responses to questions (other than when asked by bankers) regarding your personal finances. Nor should you admit, "I haven't got two nickels to rub together." The most sophisticated response to any question regarding money is something akin to, "Oh, I really can't complain," or, "We could all use more money, couldn't we?"

INFLATION

A general trend of rising prices.

INSIDER TRADING

The illegal practice of buying or selling stock based on information not available to the public. This is what so many people got in trouble for in the eighties.

IRA

An individual retirement account, which allows people to set aside money in a special account without paying taxes on it unless they withdraw funds prior to the maturity date.

MARGIN

The portion of a stock's price paid by the buyer when the broker arranges for the remainder to be purchased on credit. Buying on margin is a risky business—if the stock falls, the buyer still has to pay the amount due on the original purchase.

MUNI

A municipal bond, a debt instrument issued by a tax-exempt entity such as a state, county, city, or school district.

MORTGAGE

A legal agreement under which a specific property, usually a house, becomes the security for a loan. The creditor (bank or mortgage company) becomes the owner of the property until the loan is paid back, though the debtor usually possesses it. Large groups of mortgages also are an investment vehicle and can be traded or sold off by the creditor.

MUTUAL FUND

An investment company (or portfolio controlled by a single manager within an investment company with many funds) that invests the money of its shareholders in a diversified group of securities of other corporations. This is the hot investment of the nineties. A mutual fund can usually be opened with a small initial investment, which is attractive, as is the fact that the investors' shares in a mutual fund are invested in a variety of ways (stocks, bonds, foreign, regional, new companies, etc.), so the rise and fall of share prices isn't dependent upon the performance of any single aspect.

SECURITIES

Strictly speaking, a security is something pledged as collateral to back up a loan. In less strict terms, the word "securities" is used to signify documents (e.g., stocks and bonds) that represent claims on income or wealth.

SECURITIES AND EXCHANGE COMMISSION

More commonly known as the SEC, this is a federal regulatory agency established in 1934 to police United States securities law. The SEC's main concerns are preventing insider trading or the manipulation of stock prices.

Investing Off the Market

You don't have to put money into stocks or bonds in order to be an investor. Multitudes have accrued riches investing in nonpaper materials. Common nonsecurity investments include:

Wine

Art

Collectibles

Precious Stones

Gold

Silver

Futures

(in which one bets on future prices of commodities such as oranges and pork bellies)

Plays

(as a Broadway backer or "angel")

Motion Pictures

Restaurants

Private Companies

Real Estate

STOCK EXCHANGE

The actual buildings in which securities are bought and sold. There are seven stock exchanges in the United States. The main one is located in lower Manhattan. No one actually "drops by" the stock exchange to pick up or dump a few shares of stock, however. This is all done via computers by brokers (in return for a commission).

T-BILL

Short for treasury bill, a short-term United States government security that's not subject to state or local taxes.

TRUST

A legal arrangement in which money or property is managed by someone for the benefit of someone else. Charities and estates are often set up as trusts. Those lucky enough to be born with a trust fund usually receive either the interest from the fund, or the entire capital, upon reaching a certain age (usually twenty-one, though in spendthrift families, the dough's usually held in trust until the recipient is older and supposedly more mature).

WALL STREET

Literally, this is a small street in lower Manhattan. Figuratively, it refers to the entire range of financial networks and institutions across the country. When someone says, "Things are grim on Wall Street," they mean stockbrokers in Los Angeles or Chicago are as depressed as those in New York City.

REWARDS VERSUS RISKS IN MUTUAL FUNDS

There are five types of mutual funds. They vary in both the degree of risk involved and potential profit.

	Fluctuation in Price of Shares	Potential for Current Income	Potential for Future Income
MONEY MARKET	None	Moderate	None
INCOME	Low to moderate	High	Low
GROWTH & INCOME	Moderate	Moderate	Moderate
GROWTH	Moderate to High	Low	Moderate to High
SELECT PORTFOLIO (features stocks only in a specific industry or sector)	High	Low	High

Getting Investment Information

Maybe you can't invest yet, but you can start educating yourself now—without spending a penny. (And you know what they say about a penny saved.) It's simple, and you'll end up being much more sophisticated about finances in general.

First, contact *Morningstar's 5-Star Investor* (800/876-5005) and ask for a free sample issue of their newsletter, which rates five hundred top mutual funds.

Next, contact some of the major funds yourself through their 800 numbers (these can be found in *Morningstar* as well as in most personal finance magazines). They'll be happy to send you free information packets, which will greatly expand your knowledge of the investment process.

Some of the better-known fund brokers are Dreyfus, Fidelity, Merrill Lynch, T. Rowe, Lindner, Franklin, Scudder, and Vanguard.

Chapter Five

THE Sophisticated Aesthete

A hallmark of sophistication is the appreciation of fine art. You don't have to be a collector, just an appreciator. Nothing adds polish to a worldly demeanor more than an appreciation of art. With our handy guide, you, too, can be deemed an aesthete*—that is, one with a great understanding and appreciation of what is beautiful, especially in the arts.

The first thing you need to know is the vocabulary of art. Having the names of a few great artists at your fingertips can't hurt, either.

∼

Abstract art is art that relies on shapes, lines, and colors rather than people or things. Vassily Kandinsky is generally considered the first abstract artist for work he created in 1910.

∾

Abstract Expressionists include Willem de Kooning and Jackson Pollack, famous for dripping paint in artful designs across huge canvases. Their abstract paintings are more emotional than pure abstract art. They're also called the New York School, because that's where they hung out in the forties and fifties.

∾

Content refers to the subject matter of an artwork.

∾

Cubism is an early twentieth-century movement featuring—well, cubes. The cubists—such as Pablo Picasso and Georges Braque—painted and sculpted people and objects as a series of cubes.

∾

Dada, a silly movement everyone loves, sprang up in Zurich in 1916. The dadaists included writers and poets, and their stand was against realism. The founders—which included artists Marcel Duchamp and Max Ernst— chose the name (which is French for "hobby horse") by sticking a knife in a dictionary at random.

~

Expressionism features exaggerated and distorted images which are a reflection of the artist's emotions. The great Spanish painter El Greco is the ultimate expressionist.

~

Fauvism is the name given to the art movement created by a group of French Post-Impressionists calling themselves *Les Fauves**, French for "the wild beasts." The bold colors and broad brushwork of artists such as Raoul Dufy* and Georges Roualt* make their works a decorator's dream come true.

~

Form as an art term refers to the artist's manner of presenting various shapes that can be recognizable or abstract. (When someone says a work stresses "form over content," you can be sure it's not a painting of anything you recognize.)

~

Impressionism is one of the easiest to appreciate movements in the fine arts. Because the pastels and graceful subjects of many impressionist works are "pretty" (water lilies, ballerinas, cotton-candy-colored street scenes), it's easy to forget that when the impressionists (including Edgar Degas*, Claude Monet,* Pierre-Auguste Renoir*, and Camille Pisarro*) held their first show in nineteenth-century Paris, their works were considered shocking.

~

Minimalism is a twentieth-century movement which reduces art to its most minimal boundaries, relying solely on simple forms and flat color. Famous minimalists include Barnett Newman and Ellsworth Kelly.

~

Modern Art refers to art from the middle of the nineteenth century onward. The term usually describes art that is free of strict classical requirements and is more concerned with form than content.

~

Naïve Artists are those without formal training or those with training who purposely paint as if they haven't studied. Dounnier Rousseau's* wild jungle paintings are considered the prime example of this almost childlike art.

~

Neoclassicism was big in the late eighteenth and early nineteenth centuries and was marked by a renewed enthusiasm for classical civilization, often featuring subjects and motifs from antiquity. The Louvre in Paris has many great works by Jacques-Louis David, the neoclassicist star.

~

Neo-Impressionism is often called Pointillism* and uses dots of color to form the subject matter through "optical mixing," in which the brain involuntarily mixes juxtaposed colors to see one single hue. The Frenchman Georges Seurat* (subject of the musical *Sunday in the Park with George*) was the founder.

∼

New Realism, in vogue again, concentrates on serious portraits (that is, not often flattering). Famous practitioners include Alice Neel and Philip Pearlstein.

∼

Old Masters are distinguished artists up to the end of the eighteenth century.

∼

Op Art, popular in the sixties, features paintings based on optical illusion. Bridget Riley is one of the most well-known op artists.

∼

Photorealism describes those paintings with an almost photographic quality. Still popular today, with such artists as Chuck Close and Duane Hanson, photorealism peaked in the sixties and seventies.

∼

Pop Art usually brings to mind Andy Warhol. Started in the sixties, pop art features painting and sculpture with the look of commercial illustration and subject matter from popular culture. Roy Lichtenstein and Claes Oldenburg are other top popsters, and the Whitney Museum in Manhattan is a pantheon of pop art.

∼

Post-Impressionism is a late-nineteenth- and early-twentieth-century French movement noted for an increasing boldness in impressionistic techniques. There are some big stars here, notably Paul Cézanne*, Vincent van Gogh, and Paul Gaugin*.

Pre-Raphaelite Brotherhood is a group of mid-nineteenth-century artists, much loved by sophisticates to this day. The group—including Dante Gabriel Rossetti, John Everett Millais, and Holman Hunt—wanted to recapture the direct religiosity of Pre-Renaissance painting. The works are dramatic and romantic.

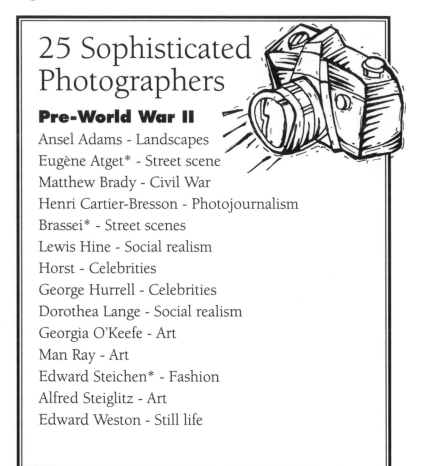

25 Sophisticated Photographers

Pre-World War II

Ansel Adams - Landscapes
Eugène Atget* - Street scene
Matthew Brady - Civil War
Henri Cartier-Bresson - Photojournalism
Brassei* - Street scenes
Lewis Hine - Social realism
Horst - Celebrities
George Hurrell - Celebrities
Dorothea Lange - Social realism
Georgia O'Keefe - Art
Man Ray - Art
Edward Steichen* - Fashion
Alfred Steiglitz - Art
Edward Weston - Still life

∼

Realism describes painting that is true to natural appearances, yet not detail-oriented. Gustave Courbet* is the founder of realism and influenced many artists. who followed.

∼

Romanticism, a nineteenth-century movement, with such famous followers as Eugène Delacroix and William Turner, featured imaginative paintings that often illustrated literary themes which are romantic in the heroic sense.

∼

Social Realism refers to the pre-1950 depiction of the ills of society. Proponents include Diego Rivera and Ben Shahn.

Post-World War II

Diane Arbus - Surreal portraits
Richard Avedon - Fashion, portraits
Elliott Erwitt - Street scenes, dogs
Annie Leibowitz - Celebrities
Robert Mapplethorpe - Still life, art (often X-rated)
Mary Ellen Mark - Photojournalism
Helmut Newton - Fashion, sadomasochistic art
Irving Penn - Still life
Herb Ritz - Celebrities, advertising
Bruce Webber - Advertising, art
William Wegman - Dogs (Weimaraners)

~

Surrealism started in the 1920s and drew on Freudian theories about the unconscious to produce imaginative works by artists including Salvador Dali and Joan Miró.

~

Symbolism, a late-nineteenth-century movement, featured erotic dream fantasies. Famous symbolists include Gustav Klimt and Gustave Moreau.

Moseying through the Museums

THE LOUVRE*
(Musee du Louvre), *Paris*

This massive edifice on the Seine's right bank presents a dazzling display of masterpieces from the past and is undoubtedly the world's greatest museum. Certainly the important painting here is Leonardo da Vinci's *Mona Lisa* (*La Giaconda* in Italian). This also is where you can see two of the most famous marble sculptures in the world: *Venus de Milo* and *Winged Victory*.

UFFIZI
(Galleria degli Uffizi), *Florence*

Michelangelo's statue of David isn't here (it's at the Academia down the road), but you will find one of the world's most important collections of Italian paintings. The "don't miss" sights include Michelangelo's

Holy Family and Botticelli's renowned gal on the half-shell, *Birth of Venus*.

RIJKSMUSEUM*
Amsterdam

No, Dutch Masters aren't cigars. They are sixteenth- and seventeenth-century master artists from the Netherlands, and this museum has an unrivaled collection of work by them, including Vermeer's *Young Woman Reading a Letter* and Rembrandt's *The Night Watch*.

METROPOLITAN MUSEUM OF ART
New York City

One of the largest and most comprehensive museums in the world is on upper Fifth Avenue. The Met's got it all, including Degas's *Dance Class* and El Greco's *View of Toledo*.

THE NATIONAL GALLERY
London

The old gray edifice in Trafalgar Square holds such masterpieces as Renoir's *Umbrellas* and Monet's *Waterlilies*. The National Portrait Gallery next door shows portraits of everyone who was anyone in the history of the United Kingdom.

PRADO
(Museo del Prado), Madrid

This Spanish building is as gorgeous as the collection it holds, which includes Breughel's *The Triumph of Death* and Goya's *Nude Maja* (usually called "The Naked Maja").

THE VATICAN MUSEUM
(Monumenti Musei e Gallerie Pontificie), *Rome*

The hot spot for holy art, this is the spot for millions of pilgrims who emerge feeling humbled by Michelangelo's breathtaking paintings on the ceiling of the Sistine Chapel (newly restored) and such famous sculptures as *Apollo Belvedere.*

NATIONAL GALLERY OF ART
Washington, D.C.

Renowned for its Chinese porcelain as well as for its collections of thirteenth- to twentieth-century European and American paintings, the National Gallery is home to Rembrandt's *Self Portrait* and Whistler's *White Girl.*

The Lives of the (Video) Artists

Want to learn more about art and artists without having to traipse through museums? Luckily, Hollywood has always felt the same way.

THE AGONY AND THE ECSTASY (1965)

Directed by Carol Reed. Starring Charlton Heston and Rex Harrison. It's a major stretch—and not just to reach the ceiling of the Sistine Chapel—as Heston plays Michelangelo.

THE MODERNS (1988)

Directed by Alan Rudolph. Starring Keith Carradine and Genevieve Bujold. This tale of Paris artists in the twenties is odd yet amusing, especially supporting actor Wallace Shawn as a Jazz Age gossip columnist.

MOULIN ROUGE (1952)

Directed by John Huston. Starring José Ferrer and Zsa Zsa Gabor. Ferrer plays Henri de Toulouse-Lautrec, the famed nineteenth-century Bohemian writer, left physically stunted yet emotionally voracious by a childhood accident.

LUST FOR LIFE (1956)

Directed by Vincente Minelli. Starring Kirk Douglas and Anthony Quinn. Douglas plays the tormented Post-Impressionist Vincent van Gogh, almost as famous for cutting off his ear as for his haunting still lifes, landscapes, and self-portraits.

CAMILLE CLAUDEL (1990)

Directed by Bruno Nuytten. Starring Isabel Adjani* and Gerard Depardieu*. This foreign film is the tragic story of twenty-one-year-old Claudel and her true-life affair with the great sculptor Rodin in late-nineteenth-century Paris.

SUNDAY IN THE PARK WITH GEORGE (1986)

Directed by James Lapine. This is the taped version of the actual stage performance of the Sondheim musical.

Mandy Patinkin plays pointillist Georges Seurat and Bernadette Peters is his mistress.

NEW YORK STORIES (1989)

Martin Scorsese* directed "Life Lessons," one of three short films. Nick Nolte plays a famous artist obsessed with assistant Rosanna Arquette and gives viewers a behind-the-scenes look at the art scene in New York's Soho.

HEARTBREAKERS (1984)

Directed by Bobby Roth. Starring Peter Coyote and Nick Mancuso. He's not nice, but he sure is sexy: Peter Coyote gives a touching and funny performance as a trendy Los Angeles artist who wants success *and* his best friend's lover.

THE HORSE'S MOUTH (1958)

Directed by Ronald Neame. Starring Alec Guinness. One of the world's greatest actors turns in a top performance as the eccentric fictional painter Gully Jimson, who causes chaos wherever he goes.

THE ARTICULATE SOPHISTICATE

aesthete (ESS-theet)
Brassei (bruh-SIGH)
Camille Pisarro (pee-SAHR-oe)
Claude Monet (moe-NAY)
Dounnier Rousseau (doon-YAY roo-SEW)
Edgar Degas (DAY-gah)
Edward Steichen (STY-kuhn)
Eugène Atget (aw-ZHAY)
Georges Roualt (zhawrzh roo-OH)
Georges Seurat (soo-RAH)
Gerard Depardieu (day-par-DOO)
Gustave Courbet (goo-STAAV koor-BAY)
Isabel Adjani (odd-JAH-nee)
Les Fauves (lay FOVE)
Louvre (LOOV)
Martin Scorcese (score-SAY-see)
Paul Cézanne (say-ZAHN)
Paul Gaugin (goh-GAN)
Pierre-Auguste Renoir (ren WAHR)
Pointillism (PWAN-te-yism)
Raoul Dufy (ra-OOL dyoo-FEE)
Rijksmuseum (RIKS-mew-say-uhm)

Chapter Six

THE *Sophisticated* Listener

Eclectic taste is the hallmark of the sophisticate where music is concerned. Jazz, rock, rap, new wave, New Age, classical, even country and western—the sophisticate can listen to almost anything except heavy metal and Muzak.

Sophisticated New Yorkers back in the thirties and forties were known as Café Society. Today's sophisticate can still be found listening to the Café Society-style singers: favorites are Bobby Short, Blossom Dearie, Frank Sinatra, Tony Bennett, Barbara Cook, Barbra Streisand, Andrea Marcovicci, Karen Akers, and Michael Feinstein.

The sophisticated ear responds strongly to mainstream jazz and classical music. Rock tastes tend toward classics of the seventies and current harder-edged groups and artists as long as they don't stray too far from the middle of the road—e.g., REM, Toad the Wet Sprocket, Suede, Concrete Blonde, and 10,000 Maniacs. And when it comes to C&W, they choose the Austin crowd (Willie Nelson, Waylon Jennings, Jerry Jeff Walker) and newer artists such as Travis Tritt, Garth Brooks, and Clint Black over traditionalists such as Dolly Parton, Tammy Wynette, Merle Haggard, and Porter Waggoner.

Sophisticates are familiar with rap because it's *au courant**, but many think listening to it is a G-Thang, as in "grueling."

The diehard sophisticate has a collection of classic 33-rpm albums, cassette tapes for the car, and CDs for playing at home.

The Late, Great Composers

Maybe classical music's not your thing. Maybe you've never tried. Regardless, knowing at least the names, general backgrounds, and some "hit tunes" of the world's greatest musical minds is a must should you be mingling with those who think no great music has been written since the nineteenth century.

EIGHTEENTH CENTURY

BRAHMS, JOHANNES*—German
German Requiem, Symphony in C Minor, Symphony No. 2 in D

BEETHOVEN, LUDWIG VAN*—Prussian
Opera *Fidelio, Symphony No. 6 in F Major* (known as "Pastoral"), *Symphony No. 9 in D Major* (known as the "Choral," or, more commonly, "Beethoven's Ninth")

BACH, JOHANN SEBASTIAN*—German
Brandenburg Concerti (1 through 6), *St. Matthew Passion,*
The Well-Tempered Clavier

HÄNDEL, GEORG FRIEDRICH*—Prussian
Messiah (oratorio), *Water Music* (suite)

MOZART, WOLFGANG AMADEUS*—Austrian
Operas include *The Marriage of Figaro, Don Giovanni, The*
Magic Flute; Symphony in G Major (known as "Jupiter")

TSCHAIKOWSKY, PETER ILYITCH*—Russian
The Nutcracker Suite, 1812 Overture

NINETEENTH CENTURY

CHOPIN, FRÉDÉRIC FRANÇOIS*—Pole
Many piano compositions, including fifty mazurkas*
and twelve polonaises*

LISZT, FRANZ—Hungarian
Hungarian Rhapsodies

MAHLER, GUSTAV—Bohemian
Symphony No. 1 in D Major

MOUSSORGSKY, MODEST*—Russian
Pictures at an Exhibition

SCHUBERT, FRANZ PETER—Austrian
Comic opera *The Magic Harp, Unfinished Symphony*
(Symphony in B Minor)

WAGNER, WILHELM RICHARD—Pole
Tannhäuser, Parsifal, The Ring of the Nibelungs
(usually called "Wagner's Ring")

TWENTIETH CENTURY

RAVEL, MAURICE JOSEPH*—Frenchman
Bolero, La Valse

STRAUSS, RICHARD—German
Opera *Der Rosenkavalier, Also Sprach Zarathustra*
("Thus Spake Zarathustra")

STRAVINSKY, IGOR—Russian
The Fire Bird, The Rite of Spring

The Boys in the Band
Instruments in a Symphony Orchestra

STRINGS double bass, cellos, violas, violins

WOODWINDS bassoons, clarinets, flutes, oboes

BRASS horns, trombones, trumpets, tuba

PERCUSSION bass drum, bells, cymbals, glockenspiel, kettledrums, snare drum, triangle, xylophone

HARPS

Opera

Opera fans are those who understand the great truth about the art form—to wit, most operas are just like *soap* operas set to music. These tales of passionate love and outright chicanery often end with one, or even all, of the participants meeting an untimely death. Because the lyrics are usually in a foreign language (Italian and German, as a rule), be sure to purchase a *libretto*, so you can follow the sordid tales in English.

Musical Notes: A Lexicon of Terms

a capella*	Singing without accompaniment
adagio*	A direction to play slowly
allegro*	A direction to play briskly
andante*	A direction to play in a moderate tempo
appassionata*	A direction to play passionately
arabesque*	A fanciful, lyrical piece of music
arpeggio*	The playing of notes in a chord successively rather than simultaneously
ballad	A narrative song
buffa	In the comic style
cantata	A piece that is sung
canto	The part of a choral work that carries the melody
chamber music	Music designed to be played in a small hall
chant	A sacred song
chord	A combination of three or more tones played at once
coda	The final passage of a piece or movement
con bravura*	A direction to play boldly
concerto	A composition designed for a single instrument, usually with orchestral accompaniment
consort	A chamber ensemble, or music written for one
counterpoint	The combination of two or more independent parts
crescendo*	A direction to increase the volume
da capo	"Take it from the top," i.e., repeat from the beginning
discord	The combination of dissonant tones
dolce*	A direction to play softly and sweetly
etude*	From the French word for "study," an exercise in technique

falsetto*	A false voice that is higher than normal range
forte*	A direction to play loudly
fortissimo*	A direction to play very loudly
harmony	The relationship of chords and their successions
impresario*	The conductor or manager of a company
libretto	The text of an opera or oratorio
mazurka	The national dance of Poland
minuet	A slow and elegant French dance
motif*	The subject of a composition
movement	A distinct division of a composition
opera	A drama set to music with scenery and costumes
operetta	A short opera
opus	A musical work
oratorio	The musical version of a scriptural text, presented without dramatic staging
pizzacato*	A direction that a stringed instrument should be plucked (rather than played with the bow)
polonaise	A stately Polish dance
reel	A Scottish dance
rhapsody	A composition of heroic character
scherzo*	A playful instrumental composition
sonata	An instrumental composition of several movements in related keys which differ in both form and character
symphony	A sonata designed to be played by an orchestra
tempo	The speed at which a piece is played
tremolo	The rapid repetition of notes to produce a trembling effect

Eight Sophisticated Operas

CARMEN
Bizet—1905

SETTING Seville, Spain

WHO LOVES Army officer Don José loves cigar-factory worker Carmen, who falls for the bull-fighter Escamillo.

WHO DIES Carmen, stabbed by Don José.

MADAME BUTTERFLY
Puccini—1875

SETTING Nagasaki, Japan

WHO LOVES Cho-Cho-San (Madame Butterfly) loves Lieutenant Pinkerton of the United States Navy, who loves—and marries—her. But then he leaves for the States, promising to return. Cho-Cho-San has a baby and patiently awaits Pinkerton's return, but he falls in love with an American and marries her.

WHO DIES Cho-Cho San, who commits hari-kari with her father's dagger.

DON QUIXOTE*
Massenet—1910

SETTING Spain

WHO LOVES The knight Don Quixote loves Dulcinea, who tells him she'll marry him if he retrieves her stolen necklace. He and his servant Sancho Panza risk death to get it back, but when Don Quixote returns it, Dulcinea laughs at him.

WHO DIES Don Quixote, crushed by Dulcinea's mockery.

SALOME*
Strauss—1905

SETTING Judaea

WHO LOVES Narraboth, captain of the guard, and Herod, tetrarch of Judaea, both love Salome, but she loves the prisoner Jokanaan.

WHO DIES Narraboth, who commits suicide; Jokanaan, who is executed after Salome demands his head on a platter; Salome, who is killed on Herod's orders because of her love for Jokanaan.

La TRAVIATA
Verdi—1853

SETTING France

WHO LOVES Alfred loves Violetta, and she loves him. But when Alfred's father begs her to give up his son for Alfred's own good, she leaves the country house they've been sharing and resumes her life in Paris. Alfred, angry and heartbroken, finds her at a party and humiliates her in front of everyone.

WHO DIES Violetta. Alfred finds out too late of her sacrifice for his sake.

TANNHÄUSER*
Wagner—1861

SETTING Medieval Germany

WHO LOVES The knight and minstrel Tannhäuser loves Elizabeth, who saves his life. But then he leaves, and Elizabeth pines away.

WHO DIES Elizabeth, as Tannhäuser is finally on his way home to her. Tannhäuser, grief-stricken when he sees Elizabeth's coffin.

AÏDA*
Verdi—1871

SETTING Egypt

WHO LOVES Aïda, an Egyptian slave in the time of the pharaohs in spite of being daughter of the King of Ethiopia, loves Rhadames, an Egyptian warrior. Rhadames is also loved by Amneris, daughter of the King of Egypt.

WHO DIES Rhadames, who is to be buried alive in an underground vault because, after a jealous Amneris has condemned him as a traitor, he refuses to marry her. Aïda, who awaits Rhadames in his tomb so they can die together.

FIDELIO
Beethoven—1905

SETTING A Spanish prison

WHO LOVES The prison porter Jacquino loves Marcellina, daughter of Roscoe the jailer. Marcellina loves her father's assistant Fidelio, not knowing Fidelio is actually Leonora, in disguise to rescue her jailed husband Florestan, an impoverished nobleman.

WHO DIES No one! Florestan is set free to rejoin Leonora, Fidelio no more, and Marcellina decides Jacquino's worth marrying, after all.

THE ARTICULATE SOPHISTICATE

a capella (ah cup-EL-ah)
adagio (ah-DAWSH-ee-oh)
Aïda (ay-EED-ah)
allegro (uh-LEG-row)
andante (awn-DAWN-tay)
appassionata (ah-pass-ee-oh-NAHT-ah)
arabesque (air-uh-BESK)
arpeggio (are-PEDGE-ee-oh)
au courant (oh koo-RAWNT)
con bravura (brah-voor-ah)
crescendo (kre-SHEN-doe)
dolce (DOLE-chay)
Don Quixote (key-HOE-tay)
etude (AY-tood)
falsetto (fall-SET-oh)
forte (FOUR-tay)
fortissimo (for-TEES-ee-moe)
Frédéric Francois Chopin (SHOW-pan)
Georg Friedrich Händel (HAN-dull)
impresario (em-press-AR-ee-oh)
Johann Sebastian Bach (bawk)
Johannes Brahms (yoh-HAH-nuhs brahmz)
Ludwig van Beethoven (BAY-toe-ven)
Maurice Joseph Ravel (raw-VEL)
mazurka (muh-ZUR-kuh)
Modest Moussorgsky (muu-SORG-skee)
motif (moe-TEEF)
Peter Ilyitch Tschaikowsky (IHL-yihch chy-KAWF-skee)
pizzacato (pizz-ah-CAUGHT-oh)

polonaise (pawl-oh-NAYS)
Salome (suh-LOH-mee)
scherzo (SKAIR-tsoe)
Tannhäuser (TAHN-hoy-zuhr)
Wolfgang Amadeus Mozart (MOTE-zart)

Chapter Seven

THE

Sophisticated
Viewer

S ophisticates love the arts, of course, especially the realm of entertainment. The ballet, the opera, the theater, and cinema (as opposed to plain old "movies") are their sustenance. This shouldn't be interpreted as meaning all sophisticates are intellectuals or that you've got to start springing for big-bucks season tickets at the Metropolitan Opera house to bone up on culture. Still, it's important to know what they think is important, and why—because what the sophisticate's eyes see, the sophisticate's mouth likes to discuss.

Television

D o sophisticated people watch the tube? By all means, though few, if any, would dream of buying one another any of those cute little "couch potato" spud pillows.

Still, if it weren't for sophisticates, public broadcasting would probably cease to exist. Those PBS T-shirts and tote bags are a giveaway, because only sophisticates ever pledge enough money to receive these premiums. The true sophisticate would prefer getting the entire schedule of the BBC (British Broadcasting Company) cabled directly to these shores, but in a pinch, there's always "Masterpiece Theater," "Absolutely Fabulous," and "Mystery."

The sophisticate's happiest TV viewing memories invariably revolve around "Upstairs, Downstairs" (taken as a whole, the series is comparable to a master's degree in the ways and wiles of the British upper classes), "Brideshead Revisited" (life among the filthy rich and greatly tortured), *Jeeves* (the misadventures of an English gentleman and his valet—rhymes with "mallet"), and "The Jewel in the Crown" (last days of the Raj, a period the British and Anglophiles* look back upon with nostalgia). Watch enough of these BBC dramas and you'll even start thinking *your* mum was presented to the Court of St. James with the rest of the debs.

If they're not watching classical concerts or BBC imports on PBS, sophisticates in front of the tube are usually hooked on (what else?) a British film being screened on the Bravo cable network.

Other than that, they turn on the television only to watch "Court TV" or the news. Sophisticates are especially fond of juicy murders and shocking scandals.

Theatre

A rudimentary knowledge of and a few quotes from Shakespeare are *de rigueur**. Other than that, sophisticates prefer contemporary playwrights who write either (1) dreary plays about the lower depths, or (2) farce or satire about sophisticated folk like themselves. They'll also grab orchestra seats (or, in London, seats in the "stalls") for revivals, preferring the very old, such as Sheridan's eighteenth-century comedy, *School for Scandal*, or works from between the World Wars.

In the first category, the dreariness of the lower depths, American David Mamet is a favorite. And if you've seen the film version of *Glengarry Glen Ross*, you'll understand just how dim a view of the world he has. Ditto, England's David Hare (and again, you can get a feel for his work at the video store, with *Plenty*). Edward Albee, author of *Who's Afraid of Virginia Woolf*, and Arthur Miller, one-time husband of Marilyn Monroe and author of *Death of a Salesman*, also are heroes.

In the second, lighter, category, Britain wins hands down with playwrights on the order of Tom Stoppard, whose *Rosenkrantz and Guildenstern Are Dead* makes even

Shakespearean tragedy seem like fun. Revivals of any Nöel Coward plays, from *Blithe Spirit* to *Private Lives*, are always hits since they deal with the thirties' and forties' cocktail crowd.

Between categories is Alan Acykborn*, an Englishman who presents a play a year in the West End, London's answer to Broadway, many of which "cross the pond." His comedies, the most famous being *Absurd Person Singular*, are filled with tragedy, his serious dramas are chock-full of laughs, so he keeps even the most

---

Beyond Broadway

Regional theater is alive and well in America and gives those who don't live in New York City the chance to see classics, current hit shows, and new plays bound for Broadway. Here are some of the most respected:

The Arena Stage, Washington, D.C.
American Repertory Theatre, Boston
Goodman Theater, Chicago
La Jolla Playhouse, La Jolla, California
Steppenwolf Theater Company, Chicago
Guthrie Theater, Minneapolis, Minnesota
Mark Taper Forum, Los Angeles

---

sophisticated playgoer confused. A fellow Brit, Simon Gray, did the same with *Butley* and *Otherwise Engaged*.

Of course, in the States, Broadway is considered the only place to experience the theater at its finest, though some regional playhouses are known for their sophisticated fare. At Broadway plays, one sits downstairs in the orchestra, upstairs in the balcony, in the middle on the mezzanine, on the side in a box, or in the front of the balcony or mezzanine in what are called loge seats. Dramas require orchestra seats, while loge seats are considered the best for viewing large-scale musicals. But then, sophisticates rarely see musicals at all, unless written by Stephen Sondheim. His *Follies*, *Company*, and *Sweeney Todd* are their favorites.

Cinema

S ophisticates catch the latest Arnold or Sly film just like the rest of us, but they don't *talk* about these. And when they do, they insist they saw it on the plane.

What sophisticates do talk about are (1) foreign films, or American films with a foreign attitude, or (2) classics.

Again, sophisticates are suckers for the British stiff-upper-lip school of entertainment, flocking to the offerings of the team of Ismail Merchant and James Ivory, most well known for *A Room with a View* and *Howard's End*.

They also like films concerning the moral dilemmas of the upwardly mobile (who often take a sudden shift in the opposite direction at some point in the film). This fare can be tragic, as in *Damage*, or comic, as in *Four Weddings and a Funeral*. And, though their own habits are pristine, they're suckers for depictions of British lowlife on the order of *Mona Lisa*, *My Beautiful Launderette*, *Naked*, and the hilarious, alcohol-saturated cult favorite *Withnail & I*.

Subtitled foreign films don't seem to be viewed by anyone *except* sophisticates. Luckily, they like the old ones the best, so even if you don't live near an art theater that screens them, you can rent obscure foreign titles at the local video shop or buy them through mail order.

The French win the foreign film sweepstakes hands down. The late François Truffaut* is the leader—his 1959 classic, *The Four Hundred Blows*, is considered the beginning of France's new wave (or *nouvelle vague*), a rebellion against the stiffness of classical filmmaking and the starting point for today's hard-edged realism. Other legendary French directors are Jean-Luc Godard (whose nihilist classic, *Breathless*, made Jean-Paul Belmondo a star) and the comic director Jacques Tati. Watch a Tati movie and you'll see why the French love Jerry Lewis.

There are two Spanish directors with whom it's worth getting acquainted. The first is Luis Bunuel*, a surrealist whose films are in French. His first film, *Le Chien Andalouse** made with Salvador Dali* was a cause celèbre because of the scene in which a woman's eyeball is sliced open on-screen; his famous tale of the corruption of the innocent, *Viridiana** , is still shocking, more than thirty years after it was made. The hot contemporary star is Pedro Almovadar*, who first won acclaim here in 1991 with his cartoonish *Woman on the Verge of a Nervous Breakdown*. Not only is he *the* Spanish director of the nineties, he's also wildly entertaining, as kinky in his own way as Bunuel was in his.

SOPHISTICATED STARS

In the eyes of the sophisticate, all movie stars are not created equal. They love some, hate some.

LOVE 'EM	HATE 'EM
Meryl Streep	Sally Field
John Malkovich	Patrick Swayze
Arnold Schwarzenegger	Sylvester Stallone
Madeleine Stowe	Madonna
Tom Hanks	Tom Cruise
Gerard Depardieu	Jerry Lewis
Susan Sarandon	Suzanne Somers
Geena Davis	Darryl Hannah
Alfre Woodard	Whoopi Goldberg
Kevin Kline	Kevin Costner
Patricia Arquette	Rosanna Arquette
Brad Pitt	David Hasselhoff
Jeff Bridges	Judd Nelson
Gary Oldman	Christopher Reeve
Bill Murray	Chevy Chase
Martin Sheen	Charlie Sheen
Sam Neill	Ryan O'Neal
Sam Shepard	Cybill Shepherd
Denzel Washington	Eddie Murphy

Sophisticates like American movies that star English actors (Emma Thompson, Kenneth Branagh, Vanessa Redgrave, Rupert Grant, Anthony Hopkins, and Jeremy Irons) or Italian-American actors (DeNiro, Pacino, Pesci). They also love offbeat character actors—Harvey Keitel, Juliette Lewis, Steve Buscemi, Johnny Depp—and like to talk about the great faces these people have.

Oddly enough, sophisticates adore really violent films, as long as they're intellectual, or extremely odd. The cultural elite flocked to *Midnight Express, Reservoir Dogs, Goodfellas, True Romance*, and *Salvador*. If you rent all the films of Martin Scorcese, Francis Ford Coppola, and Oliver Stone and make sure you don't watch them immediately after eating, you should be able to hold your own at any chic cocktail party.

For unknown reasons, a majority of sophisticated people are actually fans of Richard Gere.

The Biggest Names in Ballet

The ballet doesn't deserve the elitist image it retains in the eyes of most Americans. Admittedly, some ballets are long and drawn out, but the livelier classical ballet troupes (and many of the rousing modern dance ones) can keep a spectator as alert as a fast-paced tennis match. Whether you become a balletomane or not, you'll want to know the names of ballet legends.

ALVIN AILEY
Founder of American Dance Theater

GEORGE BALANCHINE*
The famed director and choreographer of the New York City Ballet from 1948 to 1982

MIKHAIL BARYSHNIKOV*
Leading male dancer who defected from the USSR, where he was a soloist with the Kirov Ballet

MAURICE BÉJART*
As director of the Ballet de l'Étoile in Paris, he greatly influenced dance by incorporating jazz and acrobatics

MERCE CUNNINGHAM*
Pushed modern dance to new boundaries in the fifties and sixties with his own company

JACQUES D'AMBOISE*
Former star of The New York City Ballet

AGNES DE MILLE
Dancer and choreographer famous for choreographing the Broadway musical *Oklahoma*

SERGEI DIAGHILEV*
Founder, in 1909, of the Ballet Russe in Paris, credited with revolutionizing ballet

ISADORA DUNCAN

Early-twentieth-century dancer and teacher who popularized barefoot dancers

DAME MARGOT FONTEYN*

One of the greatest stars of the Royal Ballet

MARTHA GRAHAM

American dancer and choreographer who formed her own company in 1929 and greatly influenced modern ballet

ROBERT JOFFREY

Choreographer who founded City Center Joffrey Ballet in New York City in 1954

NATALIA MARKAROVA*

Renowned ballerina with the Kirov Ballet and, later, the American Ballet Theater

VASLAV NIJINSKY*

The star dancer with Diaghilev's Ballet Russe, he is generally considered the best of the twentieth century

RUDOLF NUREYEV*

The leading classical dancer of the fifties and sixties who defected from the Kirov Ballet and danced with the Royal Ballet

ANNA PAVLOVA*
The greatest ballerina of all time, she danced with the Ballet Russe

JEROME ROBBINS
The choreographer and director of *West Side Story*

MARIA TALLCHIEF
American prima ballerina in the forties and fifties

PAUL TAYLOR
Famed dancer with both Merce Cunningham and Martha Graham companies

TWYLA THARP
A leading contemporary American choreographer

The Bard of Avon

Even if you never see, or read, any of William Shakespeare's plays, you should be familiar with their names. The Bard of Avon lived in Stratford-on-Avon in England, a town he is single-handedly responsible for making one of the top tourist spots on the map. His plays were written and produced at the Globe Theatre in the late sixteenth and early seventeenth century. Whether he wrote them all or not is a question that never goes away, as the names of several other important authors of that period have been bandied about as possible writers of several of the works.

Shakespeare's plays are divided into four categories. The most well known of each are underlined.

THE HISTORIES

<u>Henry IV, Part I</u>
Henry IV, Part II
Henry VI, Part I
Henry VI, Part II
Henry VI, Part III
<u>Richard III</u>
King John
Richard II
<u>Henry V</u>
Henry VIII

THE ROMANCES

<u>The Tempest</u>
Cymbelline
A Winter's Tale
Pericles

THE COMEDIES

The Comedy of Errors
Troilus and Cressida
Love's Labour Lost
The Two Gentlemen of Verona
<u>The Taming of the Shrew</u>

Twelfth Night
A Midsummer Night's Dream
As You Like It
Much Ado about Nothing
Measure For Measure
The Merchant of Venice
The Merry Wives of Windsor
All's Well That Ends Well

THE TRAGEDIES

Hamlet
Titus Andronicus
Romeo and Juliet
Coriolanus
Julius Caesar
Antony and Cleopatra
Othello
Timon of Athens
Macbeth

Though he wrote of kings, Shakespeare also wrote in the common language of his time about universal problems. Many of his works are available on video, and anyone who has never experienced the Bard is well advised to rent either Sir Laurence Olivier's *Hamlet* or Kenneth Branagh's *Henry V*.

Aria Addresses
The Great Opera Houses

Want to impress diehard opera fans? Just ask if they've been to the following places. Don't worry about keeping up your end of the conversation—they'll talk all night.

Teatro alla Scala—Milan, Italy
L'Opéra—Paris, France
Royal Opera House—Covent Garden, London, England
Metropolitan Opera House—New York, New York
Staatsoper* —Vienna, Austria

THE ARTICULATE SOPHISTICATE

Alan Acykborn (ACK-born)
Anglophiles (ang-glo-FILES)
Anna Pavlova (pav-LOE-vah)
Dame Margot Fonteyn (MAR-goh fawn-TAIN)
de rigueur (dih ree-GOOR)
Francois Truffaut (true-FOE)
George Balanchine (BAL-uhn-cheen)
Jacques D'amboise (zhahk dahm-BWAHZ)
Le Chien Andalouse (luh chee-ENN ahn-dah-LOOZE)
Luis Bunuel (boo-NWELL)
Maurice Béjart (bay-JAR)
Merce Cunningham (murce)
Mikhail Baryshnikov (mick-HILE buh-RISH-ne-kawf)
Natalia Markarova (mahr-kahr-OH-vah)
Pedro Almovadar (ahl-MOE-vah-dahr)
Rudolf Nureyev (NOOR-ee-ev)
Salvador Dali (DAH-lee)
Sergei Diaghilev (sehr-GAY DYAH-gih-lehf)
Staatsoper (SHTAAT-soe-puhr)
Vaslav Nijinsky (vahts-LAHF nih-ZHIHN-skee)
Viridiana (vih-rih-dee-AH-nah)

Chapter Eight

Sport

Your idea of heaven might be grabbing your bowling ball and heading down to the local lanes or hurling a few darts over some brews at your local bar. This does *not* mean you can't be sophisticated. (Actually, before pool took over, bowling was one of the 1990s' trendiest pastimes among the hip and the young.) But you've got to understand that only a few sports are considered truly to the manner born.

Sophistication is a wonderful option for those with two left feet or muscles as developed as watercress, because a sophisticate is never actually required to *play* a sport. As with other sophisticated subjects, a little lingo goes a long way.

Golf

Golfing gives sophisticates a chance to shed their starkly simple threads and don silly-looking pink, green, and madras "golf clothes." Only when choosing an ensemble for the links would anyone in his or her right mind consider Arnold Palmer a designer.

Golf's Big Five

There are numerous PGA tourneys and other golf events, but there are only five top championships.

1 *The Masters Tournament*
Played only at Augusta, where the winner is awarded a green blazer.

2 *The U.S. Open*
Rotates courses throughout the States.

3 *The British Open*
Rotates courses in Great Britain.

4 *PGA Championship*
Rotates courses in the U.S.

5 *U.S. Women's Open*
This top women's event rotates courses in the U.S.

THE SOPHISTICATED GOLF LEXICON

The proper links lingo will keep you out of the rough when conversing with a diehard golfer.

Birdie — Playing a hole in one stroke less than par.

Bogey — Playing a hole one stroke over par.

Caddy — The one who carries the clubs for a player.

Eagle — A big birdie. Playing a hole in two strokes less than par.

Fore! — Yelled to signal, "Look out, here comes the ball!"

Green — The part of each hole that comes at the end, and is immaculately smooth, with flagged cups as the final target.

Handicap — A numerical quotient assigned individual golfers in a rating system that lets golfers compete equally with one another, regardless of ability. The lower the handicap, the better the golfer. Handicaps are subtracted from scores to produce "net" scores.

Hole-in-one — Just what it says: getting the ball into the hole in a single stroke. In your dreams...

Mulligan — A free replay of a bad shot. These are usually allowed only in recreational play, but just one per round.

Par — The number of strokes a good player is expected to use to get the little ball into the hole.

Rough — The tall grass, trees, and bushes bordering fairways, someplace golfers try not to hit the ball.

Scratch Player — Has a zero handicap.

Though golfing is becoming more and more a leisure activity of the common man, it has long been associated with the elite, and is played chiefly at expensive resorts and cloistered country clubs. Even if you're not paying to play, the sport isn't cheap since the regalia consists of a whole set of clubs, a bag in which to put them, cart and caddy fees, and shoes that have no other purpose whatsoever.

The price, however, isn't the only reason golf has always been popular with the sophisticated. Power is another factor. Golf started growing to its current popularity back in the fifties, when businessmen looking to further their careers realized golfing gave them a great chance to network and make deals while ostensibly pursuing pleasure. CEOs and presidents choose the game because it offers: (1) leisurely exercise and fresh air, and (2) a chance to schmooze and do deals even on weekends.

If you'd like to learn to play golf, most public courses offer adequate lessons for beginners.

GOLF GREATS

Old golfers never die—they become pros or design courses. What did you think we were going to say?

MEN
Ben Hogan
Byron Nelson
Jack Nicklaus
Arnold Palmer
Greg Norman
Lee Trevino
Tom Watson

WOMEN
Betsy King
Nancy Lopez
Patty Sheehan
Jan Stephenson

Putter's Paradises

If someone says he or she hit the links at any of these courses, be sure to act suitably impressed.

AUGUSTA NATIONAL GOLF COURSE
Augusta, Georgia
The regulars just call it "Augusta;" everyone calls it the exclusive home of the Masters Tournament. Golf's mecca in America, Augusta is spoken of in reverent tone by golfers the world over. Known for its "Amen Corner," the decisive eleventh, twelfth, and thirteenth holes.

PEBBLE BEACH GOLF LINKS
Monterey Peninsula, California
Pebble Beach is the golf course of the stars, but the real star is the site. The immaculately manicured course is surrounded by cliffs, with not-so-gentle drops to surf-pummeled boulders. A Japanese businessman owns this course, which has gone back and forth between public and private. Nowadays, the public—at least those with the $200-a-round greens fee—is admitted. Home to the famous Pebble Beach National Pro-Am, as well as an occasional U.S. Open and other prestigious tournaments.

ROYAL AND ANCIENT GOLF COURSE
St. Andrews, Scotland

Known to golf fanatics simply as St. Andrews, this is considered the course where golf was born. In a spectacular setting, it is often the site of the British Open.

HARBOUR TOWN GOLF LINKS
Hilton Head Island, South Carolina

Harbour Town, located in a popular sophisticate's vacation spot, is known for its eighteenth hole, called the Lighthouse Hole due to the red and white lighthouse behind that green.

DORAL COUNTRY CLUB
Miami, Florida

The Doral Open and frequent PGA tournaments are played here, on what's known as the Blue Monster course because, first, it's a killer course, and, second, the grass is blue-green. This also is Arnold Palmer's "home" course.

TOUR 18
Houston, Texas

This 1992 course is a unique fantasy come true for golfers. The 200-acre site consists of holes copied from famous golf courses around the country, including Augusta's "Amen Corner" and the Blue Monster's eighteenth holes. A similar course is planned for a 1995 opening in the Dallas-Fort Worth area.

Polo

Polo is known as "the sport of kings," which makes sense, since few commoners can afford to rush out and buy a string of polo ponies. When designer Ralph Lauren wanted a name that would associate his men's clothing line with wealth, he chose "Polo." He was right on the money, since there are only a couple thousand registered players in the world. Of course, the fact that the Prince of Wales plays polo more than counterbalances Sylvester Stallone's embracing the sport.

A polo match is played between two teams of four players on horseback. There are six periods, which are known as "chukkers," of seven minutes each, with brief intermissions in between. The object: to hit the tiny polo ball with mallets and score goals.

Some animal lovers are unhappy with the sport, which was played as early as the first century A.D. Experts say that as much as 75 percent of a player's effectiveness is attributed to his mount. That's good for the player, but not so great for the horse—because of the strain on polo ponies, the same one isn't used in successive periods.

When watching a match, keep in mind that each of the four players has a specific duty: one spearheads the attack, another fights for the ball, a third (usually the strongest player) is comparable to a quarterback, and the fourth, the "back," is the defense. The pattern of play is similar to hockey or soccer.

Tennis

Tennis might seem like the most romantic game in the world, since everyone's talking about love all the time. But in this sport, "love" means "zero." Tennis has its own confusing scoring system, and "love" is just the start of it. The first point is called "fifteen,"

Tennis Talk

Make a smash with serious players by holding your own conversationally, even if you can't hold a racquet.

fault - an error, a serve that doesn't land in the designated area or a player's foot touching the court's baseline while serving.

double fault - just what it says, and for this the player loses a point

drive - a stroke made after the ball bounces (it's allowed only one bounce)

volley - a short stroke made before the ball bounces

smash - a hard overhead shot

backhand - holding the racket with the back of the hand facing out

the second is "thirty," the next is "forty," and the winning point is "game." Whenever the score is *tied* at forty, called "deuce," a player must score two more consecutive points ("advantage" and "game") to win.

If you're over thirty and have never played, the life of a fan rather than a contender is more your speed. The game is shaped by youngsters, and, like Victorian spinsters, after twenty-nine, it's just too late.

TENNIS GREATS

They came, they saw, they conquered. Some of them also had temper tantrums.

Martina Navratilova*
Pancho Gonzales*
Steffi Graf*
Monica Seles
Jimmy Connors
Billy Jean King
Boris Becker
Chris Evert Lloyd
Pete Sampras*
Andre Agassi'
John McEnroe
Arthur Ashe

Skiing

Skiing is, for many sophisticates, another chance to rush out and shop—for ski clothes, après-ski wear (for sitting in front of the fire with a cup of grog after a day on the slopes), boots, skis, goggles, hats, gloves, and a condo in Telluride. The televising of the Olympic Winter Games has encouraged more and more people to take up skiing, so most slopes around the world are mighty crowded. Skilled enthusiasts have been driven to pursue "helicopter skiing," which means they're dropped by helicopter onto virgin slopes, where the snow stretches before them in an unbroken line. However, accidents and crashes keep all but the most foolhardy or daring confined to known trails and resorts.

There are two main types of competitive skiing: alpine and nordic. Alpine skiing encompasses downhill skiing (that's right, going straight down) and slalom racing, which means skiing in a zigzag set off by flexible flagged poles. Mogul skiing is a type of slalom skiing in which the course requires the skier to pass through, or over, "moguls," which are bumps in the run. Nordic skiing refers to jumping and cross-country skiing. Cross-country skiing, a popular fitness activity, consists of skiing for longer distances on fairly flat terrain. It's this activity that fitness ski machines try to recreate.

SKI SLOPES

Ski slopes are designated by color:

GREEN—Easiest
BLUE
BLACK
BLACK DIAMOND—Most difficult

THE ARTICULATE SOPHISTICATE

Andre Agassi (AG-gah-see)
Martina Navratilova (nah-vrah-teh-LOW-vah)
Pancho Gonzales (gonn-ZAH-liss)
Pete Sampras (SAM-press)
Steffi Graf (GRAWFF)

Chapter Nine

THE Sophisticated Driver

Having the right car counts a great deal in a world where so many people judge you by appearances. But, if you've never seen the sense in splurging or had the bucks to spend upwards of $50,000 on something that is, after all, nothing more than a vehicle designed to move your body from one place to another, don't despair. You can be very sophisticated without pulling up in a Rolls Royce just by driving one of these:

ACURA NSX

Some fans say this is the most gorgeous sports car ever designed—for $70,000-plus, why shouldn't it look good?

ALFA ROMEO* SPIDER VELOCE CONVERTIBLE

Sleek, low Italian sports car.

BMW

Any car from the Bavarian Motor Works, even one long in the tooth, has a certain cachet. The new M3 will be a hot car for years to come.

CHEVROLET CORVETTE

Still classic after all these years.

DODGE STEALTH

Affordable yet waaay cool.

DODGE VIPER

An American sports car dashing enough for Europeans.

HONDA PRELUDE

Not considered as chic as it was a few years back, but still a car with a racy image.

JAGUAR* XJ6

The sportier Jags are the ones to buy after winning the lottery. The $70,000-plus XJ12 is a bit too sedate for most sophisticated tastes.

LEXUS SC300 AND SC400

The ES300, though more affordable, doesn't have the lines sophisticates love.

MAZDA MX-5 MIATA

Here's a car under $25,000 that says you're chic, daring, and a lot of fun.

MAZDA RX-7

Sophisticates especially love the standard five-speaker stereo system.

MERCEDES-BENZ* S CLASS

The S is for sophistication, but none of the cars in this class come cheap—we're talking six figures.

MITSUBISHI DIAMANTE

Not especially well known, but definitely respected.

PONTIAC FIREBIRD

Still crazy after all these years.

CARS YOU PROBABLY DIDN'T THINK OF AS SOPHISTICATED
(BUT THEY ARE)

Volkswagen Beetle
Jeep Cherokee
Old Ford Mustang or Thunderbird
'57 Chevrolet Convertible
Cadillacs with fins (but if you get a new Cadillac, people might think you're serious)
Old Datsun 280Z
Fiat Spyder
Black London taxicab
Old Checker cab
Nash Rambler

PORSCHE* CARRERA

Not only a sports car, but an accessory line. This German speedster still spells "hot stuff."

RANGE ROVER

This sports/utility vehicle's so popular in Hollywood, it practically co-starred in *The Player*. And the Queen drives one, too.

SAAB 900 SERIES

Sure, sophisticates like these cars—that's why they're known as "Snobs."

TOYOTA CAMRY

Available for under $20,000, the Camry is often called "the poor man's Lexus."

TOYOTA CELICA

Quite inexpensive but still sophisticated, especially the convertibles.

TOYOTA SUPRA

The return of this car was cheered by fast drivers.

Simply Sophisticated Transport Rules

Here are a few simple rules that help you travel in style, no matter what you're driving or riding in.

1 Don't try to fake out people you're trying to impress by parking around the corner at a restaurant or hotel where there's valet service. It just makes you look cheap.

2 Never apologize for your car (or try to pretend your Mercedes is in the shop).

3 Keep your car spotless, inside and out.

4 Don't try to impress people by renting a stretch or super-stretch limo. Both are considered flashy. If you decide to hire a car and driver, stick to a standard limo or a town car. Being sophisticated doesn't mean throwing money around.

5 Bumpers stickers aren't sophisticated. Ditch them.

6 Same thing goes for vanity plates. Do you really want the word "vanity" connected with you in people's minds?

7 If possible, opt for leather seats. And, unless you're driving a utility vehicle, restrain yourself from buying sheepskins. Sure, they're warm and comfy, but do you want to look like a gypsy cabdriver?

8 Try to refrain from calling your car anything but "the car," no matter how proud you are of your possession. There are two words for people who say "I parked the Corvette around the corner" or "We drove the Bentley down to Newport." The first is "nouveau" and the second is "rich."

9 Everyone knows it's gauche to hang a pair of fuzzy dice from the rearview mirror, but did you know the same rule applies to car deodorizers?

10 The rule for license plate holders: It's okay if they bear the name of a car dealership. Using one to announce your political opinions, sexual views, or school ties isn't just unsophisticated—in this day and age, it could be downright dangerous if you rear-end someone who disagrees with your message.

THE ARTICULATE SOPHISTICATE

Alfa Romeo (AL-fuh ro-MAY-oh)
Jaguar (JAG-waar)
Mercedes-Benz (murr-SAY-dees bens)
Porsche (POR-sha)

Chapter Ten

THE Sophisticated Reader

Sophisticated people pride themselves on their literacy. Many are actually voracious readers. Others rarely delve deeper than *The New York Times Book Review*, but not, they insist, because curling up with a book isn't their idea of a good time. "The new John Updike book sounds brilliant!" a sophisticated non-reader might groan. "If only I had the time to read!"

If you'd rather wait for the video, don't worry, reading books isn't a necessity. All that's necessary is gaining enough information to be able to carry on a conversation with a fellow sophisticate who probably hasn't read the books you're discussing, either.

What sophisticates *do* love to read are magazines. (Of course, they also read the *National Enquirer* and *The Star*, but only because "it was on the table at the garage while I was waiting for my car" or "my manicurist had it.") And they

 read newspapers, because it's pretty hard to act urbane if you have no idea what's going on in the world.

Whatever you do, don't carry around a book pretending you're reading it. Many top models do this, but they often come a cropper when someone who's actually pored over every page turns up and starts a conversation. Nothing's more embarrassing than having someone ask how you're enjoying Kafka's *The Metamorphosis* and answering, "It's a wonderful story about how people can change their lives," when it's actually about a man turning into a cockroach.

The Sophisticate's Bedside Table

While urbane folks might like to *talk* about the Great Books, they don't necessarily like to read them. Even the literati like to dip into mainstream fiction and sensational nonfiction. The sophisticate's bedside bookshelf will undoubtedly contain some of the following authors' tomes:

DOMINICK DUNNE

This popular chronicler of the jet set specializes in the *roman à clef**—that is, fiction based on thinly disguised real people. Novels such as *A Season in Purgatory* (the Kennedys) and *The Two Mrs. Grenvilles* (based on the story of a real-life *femme fatale* who fatally shot her husband) are snatched up, not just for the gossip value but because they contain all the things, names, and places sophisticates know best.

SUE GRAFTON

This mystery writer is working her way through the alphabet (*A Is For Alibi, B Is For Burglar*) and has already worked herself onto the bestseller list. The setting of her books, St. Teresa, is a thinly veiled Santa Barbara, California, and the plots often feature the foibles of the rich and sophisticated.

JOHN CHEEVER

This late master of the English language wrote about the rich, the jaded, the suburban. A great place for learning how the other half (well, the half with the Volvos) lives—especially *The Wapshot Chronicle.*

JOHN GRISHAM

His *The Firm* is a guide to upward mobility as the young hero discovers both status symbols and killers.

P. J. O'ROURKE

Brilliant, nasty, and scathingly funny, he's also a staunch Republican. What more could a sophisticate want? O'Rourke writes only nonfiction, and he's proud to be politically incorrect.

IAN FLEMING

The James Bond books aren't just great entertainment—they're also guides to the high life. Read them, and you'll request your martinis "shaken, not stirred."

JUDITH KRANTZ

They might not admit it, but sophisticates devour Krantz's bestsellers with a gusto usually reserved for caviar. Why? Because she writes about PLU (People Like Us), of course. Dining, dressing, shopping, investments—Krantz's novels are a wealth of helpful hints. *Scruples* remains her most-read book.

EVELYN WAUGH*

Okay, so he was a snob and an anti-Semite. Still, few writers have created such an enduring portrait of moneyed, cultured Brits as did Waugh (whose first name is pronounced with a hard "e"). *Brideshead Revisited* is a classic and is especially helpful to anyone who craves knowledge of Oxbridge. ("Oxbridge" is used by the British to define the environment of both Oxford and Cambridge Universities, advanced learning centers for Britain's blue bloods.) It says much about England that Waugh's books, though written in the thirties, are not terribly outdated in describing upper-class life.

DONNA TARTT

Her 1993 bestseller, *The Secret History*, is a "philosophical mystery" about preppy college students gone wrong.

LISA BIRNBAUM

Ten years after its publication, her *Preppy Handbook* is still the reliable source for those who emulate the Bushes and the Gores.

The Sophisticated Subscriber

Here are the daily, monthly, and weekly journals the sophisticate depends upon for keeping abreast of news.

Allure	*Premiere*
Condé Nast Traveler*	*Spy*
Details	*The Atlantic Monthly*
Forbes	*The New York Times*
Gourmet	*The New Yorker*
Harper's Bazaar	*The Wall Street Journal*
Interview	*Time*
New York	*Vanity Fair*
Newsweek	*Vogue*
People	*W*

How the Other Half Lived
Classics of Sophistication

Reading the following books will stir your imagination, refine your manners, and allow you to hold your head high amongst the *literati**. (All are available in video for those who consider this book the heaviest reading they're willing to consider.)

PRIDE AND PREJUDICE
The urbane and intelligent Elizabeth Bennet and Fitzwilliam Darcy fall in love in Jane Austen's 1913 novel.

VANITY FAIR
The strong-willed Becky Sharpe is considered one of the great comic creations in literature, and after reading William Makepeace Thackeray's 1848 classic, you'll know why.

TOM JONES, A FOUNDLING
Henry Fielding's great eighteenth-century comedy deals with hypocrisy, love, and lust amongst the landed gentry. If you don't read the book, at least rent the movie, starring the young Albert Finney.

ANNA KARENINA
The Kareninas are one of Russia's elite, but life takes a tragic turn for Anna when she falls in love with a dashing count who's not her husband in Leo Tolstoy's 1877 masterpiece.

THE MOST SOPHISTICATED WRITERS OF THE 20th CENTURY

A double asterisk means there's a movie version for non-readers.

Baldwin, James	*Another Country* (1962)
Beattie, Ann	*Chilly Scenes of Winter*** (1976)
Bellow, Saul	*Herzog* (1964)
Bradbury, Ray	*Fahrenheit 451*** (1953)
Burroughs, William	*Naked Lunch*** (1959)
Chandler, Raymond	*The Big Sleep*** (1939)
Cheever, John	*The Wapshot Chronicle* (1957)
Didion, Joan*	*Play It As It Lays* (1970)
Doctorow, E.L.	*Ragtime*** (1975)
Dreiser, Theodore*	*An American Tragedy***
Faulkner, William	*The Sound And The Fury* (1929)
Fitzgerald, F. Scott	*The Great Gatsby*** (1925)
Hammett, Dashiell	*The Maltese Falcon*** (1930)
Heller, Joseph	*Catch-22*** (1961)
Hemingway, Ernest	*A Farewell To Arms*** (1929)
Jong, Erica	*Fear of Flying* (1973)
Kerouac, Jack	*On The Road* (1957)
Kosinski, Jerzy*	*Being There*** (1971)
McCarthy, Mary	*The Group*** (1963)
Plath, Sylvia	*The Bell Jar*** (1963)
Roth, Philip	*Portnoy's Complaint* (1969)
Styron, William	*Lie Down In Darkness* (1951)
Tyler, Ann	*The Accidental Tourist*** (1985)
Updike, John	*Rabbit, Run*** (1960)
Vonnegut Jr., Kurt*	*Slaughterhouse-Five*** (1969)
Walker, Alice	*The Color Purple*** (1982)

THE PORTRAIT OF DORIAN GRAY

Not only is he the most dazzling young man in London society, but handsome Dorian Gray never looks a day older, no matter how much he drinks or how many drugs he takes. Strange, isn't it? Oscar Wilde's 1891 portrait of debauchery is still fun and fascinating.

The Great British Poets

GEOFFREY CHAUCER

His medieval masterpiece, *The Canterbury Tales*, is still a good read if you've got a modern translation.

EDMUND SPENSER

His sixteenth-century *The Faerie Queen* is considered the quintessential English Renaissance poem.

WILLIAM SHAKESPEARE

His sonnets are as renowned as his plays.

JOHN DONNE

He is considered the greatest of the seventeeth-century poets.

JOHN MILTON

He wrote the classic *Paradise Lost* in the eighteenth century.

THOMAS GRAY

You probably read this eighteenth-century poet's *Elegy in a Country Churchyard* in school.

WILLIAM BLAKE

This nineteenth-century prophetic poet is famous for *Jerusalem.*

LORD BYRON

George Gordon, the nineteenth-century Romantic poet, also penned some wild diaries; *Childe Harold's Pilgrimage* and *Don Juan* are his most famous poetic works.

JOHN KEATS

This former medical student wrote many odes in the early nineteenth century.

PERCY BYSSHE SHELLEY

This nineteenth-century poet wrote the verse drama *Prometheus Unbound* and married Mary Goodwin, who, as Mary Shelley, wrote *Frankenstein.*

WILLIAM WORDSWORTH

This nineteenth-century poet lived in England's beautiful Lake District and wrote tributes to the beauty of nature.

ROBERT BROWNING

The husband of writer Elizabeth Barrett Browning was the author of such powerful poems as *My Last Duchess.*

ALFRED TENNYSON

His late-nineteenth-century *Idylls of the King* is considered the most powerful retelling of Arthurian legends.

THE ARTICULATE SOPHISTICATE

Condé Nast Traveler (KON-day)
Evelyn Waugh (WAW)
Jerzy Kosinski (koe-ZEN-skee)
Joan Didion (DID-ee-un)
Kurt Vonnegut, Jr. (VAWN-uh-gut)
literati (lit-uh-ROTT-ee)
roman à clef (roe-MAWN ah KLAY)
Theodore Dreiser (DRY-zer)

Chapter Eleven

THE
Sophisticated
Linguist

Sophisticates might seem snobbish and affected when they start throwing foreign phrases at one another, but truthfully there are times when saying it in another language says it best of all—even better than saying it with flowers.

Our own language is a hybrid that's evolved from many different foreign roots. And, as jet travel makes the world a smaller place, one often finds oneself conversing with someone who uses foreign terms as casually as Valley Girls say, "It was, like, awesome." In other countries, and among the upper levels of our own society, classical languages (i.e., Latin and Greek) are still studied, and it's not unusual for a worldly person to speak four, five, six, even seven other tongues.

You, too, can learn to speak many languages in minutes, thanks to this chapter, which will give you phrases that can lounge on the tip of your tongue, waiting for the right time to slide off.

Latin
It's Not Dead Yet

We use Latin every day, often without knowing it. The following twenty Latin phrases are guaranteed to add a touch of class to your conversation. Since many of the "proper" Latin pronunciations aren't heard outside the classroom (for example, the letter "v" is pronounced as a "w" in classical Latin, but you'll rarely hear it that way in everyday use), the pronunciations here are those that will mark you as a worldly person rather than a pedant.

AD INFINITUM
ad in-fi-NIGH-tum   endlessly, to infinity

AD NAUSEUM
ad NAW-see-um   to the point of nausea or disgust

AD HOC
ad HOCK   impromptu

A PRIORI
ah pree-OH-ree   deduced from reasoning rather than experience

CAVEAT EMPTOR
KAY-vay-aht EMP-tor   Let the buyer beware

NON COMPOS MENTIS
non KOM-pos MEN-tis   not of sound mind

DE FACTO
day FAK-toe   a fact rather than a choice

IN VINO VERITAS
in VEE-no VER-i-tas   Literally means "in wine there is truth." In other words, drunks don't lie.

MEMENTO MORI
me-MEN-toe MO-ree   A reminder of the fact that one is mortal

MODUS OPERANDI
MO-dus op-er-AND-ee   method of operating, or, as the police say, M.O.

NE PLUS ULTRA
ne ploos UL-tra   the best or highest point possible; the bee's knees

O TEMPORA, O MORES!
oh TEM-po-rah, oh MOR-ays   "Oh, the times, Oh, the manners." Used to say things are changing greatly and not for the best

QUID PRO QUO
kwid proh KWOH   getting something in return for giving something; tit for tat

SUB ROSA
sub ROE-sah   in secret

TEMPIS FUGIT
TEM-pus FEW-jit   time flies

VOX POPULI
vox POP-you-lee   public opinion

Parlez-Vous Français?

The average sophisticate is in awe of France, deeming it the world's most sophisticated country. Whether you chalk this up to absolute fact or to fools buying the Parisians' hype, French is the language *les femmes et les hommes du monde** (men and women of the world) love to throw around.

À BIENTÔT!
an BYEN-toe   See you soon!
                                     "I've got to run. But let's
                                     meet again for espresso
                                     next week. À bientôt!"

AFFAIRE DE COEUR
ah-FAIR de KUHR   love affair
                                     "Nothing wrong with me
                                     that a good affaire de coeur
                                     wouldn't cure."

À TOUT PRIX

ah too PREE

at any price
"I must have that cashmere sweater. À tout prix!"

BEAU MONDE

bow MOHND

society, the jet set
"I like to consider myself sophisticated, but I'm certainly not a member of the beau monde."

BON APPÉTIT

bone AP-peh-tee

Enjoy your meal. (literally, "Good appetite")
"Don't these escargots look scrumptious? Mmnnn, bon appétit!"

C'EST LA GUERRE

say lah GARE

So it goes. (literally, "That's war")
"She got married again a week after our divorce. Ah, well, c'est la guerre!"

CHACUN SON GÔUT

shack-UN son goo

each to his own taste
"Are you serious? You prefer Far Rockaway to the Hamptons? Chacun son gôut, I suppose."

COMME SI, COMMI ÇA

com SEE com SAH

so-so
"How did I like the Jerry Lewis movie? Comme si, comme ça."

COMME IL FAUT

comb eel FOE

socially acceptable
"Forget it's a biker bar and go on in. It's very comme il faut this year."

NOBLESSE OBLIGE

no-BLESS oh-BLEEJE

The rich and powerful must take responsibility.
"The Moneybucks have been very supportive of our charity auction. They have a real sense of noblesse oblige."

CRÈME DE LA CRÈME

KREM deh lah krem

the best
"You've got to have dinner at Union Square Cafe when you're in New York. It's the crème de la crème."

PLUS ÇA CHANGE, PLUS C'EST LA MÊME CHOSE

ploo sah shahnje, ploo say lah mem shose

The more something changes, the more it stays the same.
"Does it matter if the GOP or the Democrats win? It's always plus ça change, plus c'est la même chose."

TOUR DE FORCE

TOOR deh force

display of great skill
"Would you agree that *King Lear* is Shakespeare's tour de force?"

Raise Your Glass Around the World

Do you always wish you had something besides "Here's how!" or "Cheers!" to say when raising a glass in a toast? Foreign phrases are always acceptable in chic circles, even when no one knows what they mean.

À VOTRE SANTÉ!
Ah vau-truh sawn-TAY

French
"To your health!"

BANZAI!
Bahn-ZY

Japanese
"May you live for ten thousand years!"

A VUESTRA SALUD!
ah VWES-trah sa-LOOD

Spanish
"To your health!"

SALUTE!
sah-LOO-teh

Italian
"To your health!"

CIN CIN!
cheen cheen or *chin chin*

Italian toast also heard in Britain
"Cheers!"

SKOAL!
skole

Danish
Literally means "Cup," so "Bottoms up!" is the best translation.

L'CHAIM
le khime

Hebrew
"Long life!"

THE ANGLOPHILE'S ABCs

It's sophisticated to know Britishisms and okay to use them
when speaking to a Brit. When addressing a fellow Yank, stick
to the U.S. vernacular or risk being branded "affected."

ENGLISH	BRITISH
apartment	flat
appetizer	starter
broke (money-wise)	skint
bus	coach
candy	sweets
corn	maize
cutesy	twee
dessert	pudding
drugstore	chemist's
elevator	lift
flashlight	torch
gasoline	petrol
hood (car)	bonnet
lavatory	loo
line (the kind one stands in)	queue
newsstand	bookstall
nosepoke (busybody)	nosey parker
oven	cooker
penny-pinching	cheese-paring
reservation	booking
sneakers	plimsolls
squash	marrow
stink	pong
subway	underground
tote bag	Dorothy bag
truck	lorry
trunk (car)	boot
vest	waistcoat
water heater	geyser
worthless	naff

Ten Sophisticated Abbreviations

GOP—This stands for Grand Old Party, and it means Republican, as in, "I'm a liberal at heart, but since I've started investing heavily, my head belongs to the *GOP*."

HRH—The shortened form of His/Her Royal Highness, used in writing as opposed to speaking, as in "*HRH* Prince Charles requests your company for dinner." Don't you *wish*?

c., ca.—Usually used only in written form, this is the abbreviation for the Latin word *circa*, meaning "about." For example: "Just a quick note, since I've been working so hard my last day off was *c.* 1983."

k —Short for one thousand, as in "I heard she's getting paid 100*k* a year."

i.e.—Another Latinate abbreviation, short for *id est*, or "that is." This is used in writing, as in, "I wouldn't go out to dinner with you if you were the last man in the world—*i.e.*, drop dead."

e.g.—The full Latin phrase is *exempli gratia*, which means "for example." For example: "He always brought her an exquisite piece of jewelry, *e.g.*, from Tiffany or Cartier."

pro tem—This (Latin again) stands for *pro tempore*, and means "for the time being." For example: "Bill was elected chairman *pro tem* of the fraternity reunion committee."

R.—The Latin abbreviation for King (*rex*) or Queen (*regina*), as in "Elizabeth R."

RIP—The Latins said a mouthful—*requiescat in pace*—which means "Rest in peace." You might say, "Fortunately, that relationship is over, *RIP*."

P & L—We're talking "*profit and loss* [statement]" here, a subject that can strike terror or cause joy to course through a sophisticated entrepreneur's heart when the prospective investor says, "Before I can agree to finance your new Trends for the Trendy Report, I'll need to see a detailed *P & L*."

THE ARTICULATE SOPHISTICATE

les femmes et les hommes du monde (lay fomme ey laze owm due MOHNDE)

Chapter Twelve

THE
Sophisticated
Traveler

Travel broadens the minds, even if it thins the wallet, so sophisticates love to go anywhere and everywhere as often as possible. Sophisticated vacations include: wardrobe and accessories shopping in Europe; exploring the inns of Bucks County; antique-hunting in New England; flying to Milan to go to the opera; listening to symphonies in Santa Fe; playing *baccarat* in Monte Carlo; jetting to London for theater nights in the West End; soaking up the sun on a Caribbean cruise; piling up the pasta throughout Italy; and steaming off the pounds at spas. Unsophisticated vacations include staying home to work on the house and taking the family to Disney World.

Around the World in Eighty Seconds

You don't have to leave the country, or even your hometown, to nod knowingly when Jim and Joan Jet Set start gushing about their last vacation. Just use our handy guide to global hot spots.

ROME, ITALY

The Colosseum, built in A.D. 75, where the gladiators fought. St Peter's, in the Vatican, the most important Catholic church in the world.

VENICE, ITALY

The Grand Canal and the small canals which traverse the city, traveling by *vaporetto* (the boat "bus") or the classic *gondola*. St. Mark's Cathedral. The Bridge of Sighs, a sixteenth-century bridge through which the condemned would pass on their way to their death.

FLORENCE, ITALY

The Uffizzi Museum, with the world's greatest collection of Renaissance art. Il Duomo, built in 1296 by Brunelleschi, with the largest dome in Christendom and striped marble walls.

PARIS, FRANCE

Left bank (Rive Gauche) of the Seine: the Eiffel Tower; Notre Dame Cathedral, built in 1163 and the site of Napoleon's coronation; The Latin Quarter's sidewalk cafés. Right bank (Rive Droit): The Champs Elysees, a spacious boulevard; the Arc de Triomphe; the Louvre.

LONDON, ENGLAND

The Houses of Parliament on the River Thames (tems), with the famous "Big Ben" clock on top. Buckingham Palace and the Changing of the Guard. The Tower of London (where the Crown Jewels are displayed).

EDINBURGH, SCOTLAND

The Royal Mile, which runs through the medieval quarter. The Chapel of St. Margaret, built in 1076.

TOKYO, JAPAN

The seventeenth-century Imperial Palace. The Ginza shopping district. The tallest metal tower in the world, the Tokyo Tower.

MOSCOW, RUSSIA

The River Volga. Red Square. The Bolshoi Theatre of Opera and Ballet.

RIO DE JANEIRO, BRAZIL

Sugarloaf Mountain and Copacabana Beach. World-famous for its Carnival during Mardi Gras.

Ten Sure Signs You're in a Sophisticated Hotel

1 There is a concierge* or hall porter to help with your faxes, dinner reservations, theater tickets, etc.

2 The floral arrangements on lobby tables are more than three feet high.

3 The amenities in your bathroom are plentiful and upscale rather than plain old Vidal Sassoon.

4 Guest rooms have two-line telephones and/or a phone extension in the bathroom.

5 The bathroom has its own blow dryer attached to the wall.

6 Everyone at the hotel knows your name and refers to you as Ms. So-and-So or Mr. Such-and-Such.

7 There are terrycloth robes in the closet for use during your stay.

8 No one runs a vacuum cleaner outside your door at 7:00 A.M.

9 The television, clock, and lamps aren't bolted down.

10 Hangers are wooden and can be removed from the closets.

AMSTERDAM, THE NETHERLANDS

Canals and museums (Rembrandt's house, the Rijksmuseum, the Van Gogh Museum). The Anne Frank House.

HONG KONG

A British Crown Colony on a ninety-nine-year lease, Hong Kong will be restored to China on July 1, 1997. The gateway to China, the city is a banking and shopping capital. The Temple of Ten Thousand Buddhas actually contains more than ten thousand of them.

THE WITTIEST TRAVEL WRITERS

Maybe you can't travel as much as you'd like, but you can experience the adventures and misadventures of three very funny—and wryly sophisticated—men.

Paul Theroux* - He's crotchety, he's opinionated, and thank goodness he's written so many books and journeyed everywhere from Siberia *(The Great Railway Bazaar)* to Patagonia *(The Old Patagonian Express)*.

Bill Bryson - Born in Des Moines, living in London, he's got American adventurousness combined with British sarcasm. *The Lost Continent* details his uproarious drive around America, while *Neither Here Nor There* sees him flailing around Europe.

P. J. O'Rourke - He travels to the world's worst places and says even worse things about them. His *Holidays In Hell* is definitely non-PC and definitely hilarious.

COPENHAGEN, DENMARK

The twenty-acre Tivili Gardens, an amusement park with lakes, gardens, and restaurants. The Stroget, a one-mile-long pedestrian thoroughfare lined with shops.

THE WORLD'S MOST SOPHISTICATED HOTELS

Unless your Great Uncle Harry left you unexpected lucre in his will, you may not be staying at these upscale hostelries. But you'll want to make sure you act suitably impressed when others tell you they did.

Grand Bretagne*, Athens
Brenner's Park Hotel, Baden-Baden
Shepheard's Hotel, Cairo
Majestic, Cannes
Peninsula, Hong Kong
Halekulani*, Honolulu
Connaught*, London
Bel Air Hotel, Los Angeles
Ritz, Madrid
Carlyle , New York City
The Breakers, Palm Beach
Crillon*, Paris
Excelsior, Paris
Hassler-Villa Medici*, Rome
Grand Hotel, Stockholm
Gritti Palace, Venice
Imperial, Vienna
Baur au Lac*, Zürich

MADRID, SPAIN

The twenty-eight-hundred-room Royal Palace. The Prado Museum.

VIENNA, AUSTRIA

The Gothic St. Stephen's Cathedral. The Hofburg Palace. The four-hundred-year-old Spanish Riding School.

BOMBAY, INDIA

The Hanging Gardens. Chowpatty Beach.

BEIJING, PEOPLE'S REPUBLIC OF CHINA

The Forbidden City, where the emperor once lived. Tian'anmen Square.

SYDNEY, AUSTRALIA

The Sydney Opera House, built in 1957, which has been likened to a giant seagull and a flying nun. Bondi Beach, considered by many to be the best in the world.

MEXICO CITY, MEXICO

The ornamental Altar of the Kings inside the massive Cathedral of Mexico (sixteen chapels, twenty-seven altars). The Great Temple of Tenochitlan, considered the greatest archeological find of the twentieth century.

MONTREAL, CANADA

Vieux Montreal, the oldest section of the city. The Assemblée Nationale, Quebec's parliament.

MUNICH, GERMANY

The Deutsches Museum, the world's largest science and technology museum. The view of the Alps from the three-hundred-foot tower at Alte Peter Kirche, the city's oldest church. Dachau Concentration Camp, now a memorial, where more than two hundred thousand people were imprisoned by the Nazis during World War II. Munich is home to Oktoberfest, a sixteen-day celebration in late September famous for ever-flowing beer.

Islands in the Sun

The sophisticated traveler is a sunbird who uses a strong SPF but still loves to follow the sun, and is especially content to be surrounded by water. Herewith, some islands that are hot in more ways than one.

CARIBBEAN (AND VICINITY) ISLANDS

Anguilla*
Antigua*
Barbados
Bermuda
Mustique*
St. Barthélemy (St. Barts)
St. John, United States Virgin Islands
St. Lucia
Tortola, British Virgin Islands
Cayman Islands
Turks and Caicos

HAWAIIAN ISLANDS

Oahu* (Honolulu)
Hawaii (The Big Island)
Maui*
Kauai*
Lanai*
Molokai*

OTHER ISLANDS

Bali
Canary Islands, Spain
Fiji - Actually a republic of many small islands eleven
hundred miles from Auckland, New Zealand
Ionian Islands, Greece
Isle of Man, United Kingdom
Key West, Florida

Mackinaw* Island, Michigan
Majorca*, Spain
Martha's Vineyard, Massachusetts
Nantucket, Massachusetts
Sanibel* Island, Florida
Santa Catalina, California
Sardinia, Italy
Tahiti
Vancouver Island, British Columbia, Canada

Ten Tips for First-Time Cruisers

Many sophisticated travelers prefer to journey *in* their rooms rather than flitting from one hotel to another. Today, booking a cruise is considered quite the thing to do, as cruise ships have "hipped up" their image and cruising is no longer relegated to the realm of "the newly wed and the nearly dead." If you're planning your first cruise, these tips should help you.

1 Cruises vary from cruise line to the type of cruise. Ask around and don't make your decision based only on cost and destinations. No matter what kind of crowd you're looking for—young, old, party hearty, super-sophisticated—there's a ship and a route for you.

2 People have been cruising for pleasure only about one hundred fifty years, in which time cruise ships have come to resemble huge resorts more than boats. If you *really* want to experience the sea more than the amenities of a floating hotel, contact one of the sailing vacation companies such as Windjammer Cruises.

3 Prepare to pay according to cabin location as well as cabin size and view. The higher the deck, the higher the cost—an expense many seasoned travelers feel isn't worth the price.

4 In spite of high-tech stabilizers that greatly minimize the huge ships' roll, if the weather's rough, people do get seasick. If you're prone toward motion sickness, try to get a cabin as close to the center of the ship as possible.

5 Travel light. You must stow your luggage in your stateroom, and, other than the most expensive bookings, staterooms could be called "smallrooms."

6 Though meal service is inclusive in the price, wine and liquor are extra, so be careful how lavishly you order these. Many lines allow you to purchase duty-free alcohol at ports of call for imbibing in the privacy of your room.

7 Don't worry about tipping. You don't tip anyone until the end of the cruise, and you will be given guidelines to help determine who should get how much.

8 Captains no longer have the authority to perform marriages. You can judge for yourself if that's good or bad news.

9 You can usually save money if you book your cruise very early or very late. (Reference, *Never Say "Hi, Jack!" in an Airport*, by Terry Denton)

10 Complaints? See the purser.

Spas
Exhilarating and Expensive

The emphasis on fitness has made spas top destination resorts for the sophisticated. The financially well-endowed drop three thousand dollars a week or more at places like Maine Chance and The Golden Door, the executive class purchases pampering at La Costa and Doral Saturnia, and even those with limited funds can head for The Ashram or Rancho La Puerta.

What can you expect on a spa vacation? Delicious meals that are low in calories, fat grams, and size of portions; early morning hikes; facials and massage; relentless

Three European Restaurants Worth the Splurge

LA TOUR D'ARGENT*
Paris

Pilgrims from every corner of the globe come to pay homage, especially to one of the world's greatest wine lists. The ground floor bar is where the rich and famous converge to sip *apéritifs*, while the dining room above offers to-die-for views of Notre Dame.

ENOTECA PINCHIORRI*
Florence

Bring your platinum card when you dine in the lush garden courtyard of this Renaissance palace, once the home of fifteenth-century navigator Verazzano.

LE CAPRICE*
London

The decor is spare and modern, the food tends toward the *nouvelle*, and open tables are scarce as hens' teeth unless you book far in advance. When you do get in, don't be surprised to spot Princess Diana or Jeremy Irons across the room, because this is where show business and blue blood mingle.

aerobics' trainers; and all the comforts of an upscale sanitarium. The more you pay, the less you'll actually have to work (as in work *out*). The most luxurious spas are for the rich, who prefer pampering to physical abuse. The lower-priced spas are for Spartans and fitness fanatics.

European spas also are in vogue with Americans. Those in Germany, France, and Italy boast mineral springs and are usually singled out for the curative reputation of their waters. These European spas are regal and worldly—in Baden-Baden, Germany, for instance, spa-goers can dress up in the evening for concerts and the casino. British spas are, in keeping with the British approach to health, on the dour side, with lots of emphasis on high colonics and fasting—all suffered through in beautiful old country-house surroundings.

Traveling in (Very High) Style

T oday, when, thanks to the preponderance of business travelers, first-class upgrades have become common, there remain three very uncommon and exclusive modes of long-distance transport.

QUEEN ELIZABETH 2

The QE2, as the last of the great transatlantic ocean liners is known, celebrated her twenty-fifth birthday in 1994. This 66,000-ton luxury liner is the flagship of Britain's

Cunard Lines and the undisputed queen of 1990s' seas. There are more than nine hundred cabins on this seagoing grand hotel, which sails the Caribbean in addition to circling the globe. QE2 voyages are noted for such perquisites as hiring the personal chefs to monarchs and heads of states for some segments of the three-month world cruise. The full world cruise doesn't come cheap. Prices range from $23,000 to $145,000 per person based on double occupancy. A special deal ("special" is still more than five grand) lets passengers sail one-way to Paris on the QE2 and fly home on the Concorde.

ORIENT EXPRESS

This legendary train, the full name of which is the Venice Simplon Orient-Express, resumed luxury service in 1982, after a five-year hiatus. Noted for lavishness and extravagant ticket prices, the Orient Express is decorated with an opulence that recalls its heyday in the earlier part of the century. Popular routes include the sleeper train from London to Venice and the Paris-Venice-Vienna run. Price? For longer trips, if you have to ask, don't start packing. Tickets run in the thousands of dollars.

CONCORDE

For approximately $7,000 round-trip, you can cut the flying time between New York and London or Paris in half, by flying the 1,350-mile-per-hour Concorde, operated only by Air France and British Airways. Expensive? Yes. But every Concorde one-hundred-seat flight is almost always sold out. A bit noisier than a 747, the Concorde flies smoothly, without even a jolt to the passengers as the plane breaks the sound barrier and climbs to a streaking altitude of fifty-three thousand feet.

THE ARTICULATE SOPHISTICATE

Anguilla (ahn-GWEE-lah)
Antigua (ahn-TEE-gwah)
Baur au Lac (BOWR-owe-lock)
concierge (kohn-see-AIRJE)
Connaught (kah-NAWT)
Crillon (cree-YOHN)
Enoteca (ee-noh-TEK-kah) Pinchiorri (pin-chee-ORR-ree)
Grand Bretagne (breh-TAHN-yah)
Halekulani (hah-lay-koo-LAH-nee)
Hassler-Villa (vee-lah) Medici (MAY-dee-chee)
Kauai (kuh-WHY)
Lanai (lay-NIE)
La Tour d'Argent (lah TOOR dar-ZHAWN)
Le Caprice (leh kah-PREECE)
Mackinaw (MACK-in-nack)
Majorca (mah-YOR-kah)
Maui (MAO-wee)
Molokai (MAH-lah-kie)
Mustique (muss-TEEK)
Oahu (oh-AH-hoo)
Paul Theroux (theh-ROO)
Sanibel (SAH-nih-bell) Island